Modern Critical Interpretations

Erich Maria Remarque's
All Quiet on the Western Front

Edited and with an introduction by
Harold Bloom
Sterling Professor of the Humanities
Yale University

D0075315

CHELSEA HOUSE PUBLISHERS
Philadelphia

Printed and bound in the United States of America

10 9 8 7 6 5 4 3 2

∞ The paper used in this publication meets the minimum
requirements of the American National Standard for
Permanence of Paper for Printed Library Materials,
Z39.48-1984

Library of Congress Cataloging-in-Publication Data

All Quiet on the western front / editor, Harold Bloom.
        p. cm. — (Modern critical interpretations)
    Includes bibliographical references (p.) and index.
    ISBN 0-7910-5923-5 (alk. Paper)
    Remarque, Erich Maria, 1898–1970. Im Westen
nichts Neues. I. Bloom, Harold. II. Series.

PT2635.E68 Z55   2000
833'.912—dc21   00-060320
                           CIP

www.chelseahouse.com

Contributing Editor: Pamela Loos

Produced by: Robert Gerson Publisher's Services, Santa Barbara, CA

Modern Critical Interpretations

Contents

Editor's Note

My Introduction ponders the question of the aesthetic merits of Remarque's first and best novel, while acknowledging its historical importance as anti-war fiction.

William K. Pfeiler complains that *All Quiet on the Western Front* is a sentimental work of self-pity, while Edwin M. Moseley contrasts D. H. Lawrence and Wilfred Owen to Remarque as portrayers of Christ as a doomed youth.

Hemingway's *A Farewell to Arms* is compared by Helmut Liedloff to Remarque's war novel, after which Wilhelm J. Schwarz explores the startling difference between Remarque's hatred of war and the exaltation of battle by Ernst Jünger.

Remarque's bestseller is contextualized by A. F. Bance in the perspectives of the later 1920s, while Christine R. Barker and R. W. Last give a comprehensive survey of the early critical reactions to the book.

For Roland Garrett, Remarque's novel is an ironical version of educational experience, after which Hans Wagener locates *All Quiet on the Western Front* in the context of Remarque's literary career.

In this volume's final essay, Brian O. Murdoch sees the novel as a continuous study of loss, so that the protagonist, Paul Bäumer, is virtually stripped of everything inward before he is killed.

Introduction

*A*ll *Quiet on the Western Front* was first published in book form in 1929, and was translated soon after into English. It was Erich Maria Remarque's third novel, and has always remained his most popular, though several of his later works were very successful with the public in the 1940s and 1950s. But his other books have faded away, and now are scarcely readable. *All Quiet on the Western Front* remains very popular and is widely read, but whether it is more than another period piece seems quite questionable to me.

As a literary critic I have always tried to follow Dr. Samuel Johnson, who warned that contemporary literary fame has a way of vanishing:

> Of many writers who filled their age with wonder, and whose names we find celebrated in the books of their contemporaries, the works are now no longer to be seen, or are seen only amidst the lumber of libraries which are seldom visited, where they lie only to show the deceitfulness of hope, and the uncertainty of honour.
>
> Of the decline of reputation many causes may be assigned. It is commonly lost because it never was deserved, and was conferred at first, not by the suffrage of criticism, but by the fondness of friendship, or servility of flattery. The great and popular are very freely applauded, but all soon grow weary of echoing to each other a name which has no other claim to notice, but that many mouths are pronouncing it at once.

Let me add, to the great Samuel Johnson, the sublime Oscar Wilde with his two critical adages: everything matters in art, except the subject, and all bad literature is sincere. What matters most in *All Quiet on the Western Front* indeed is the subject, Word War I, and the book is very sincere. It is therefore not a work of art, but a period piece and a historical document.

1

To be even more autobiographical, I discovered recently how much fury can be generated by naming a currently popular work as just another period piece. After I discussed the Harry Potter fad in the *Wall Street Journal*, the *Journal* received eighty negative letters and none positive. J. K. Rowling, like Stephen King and Danielle Steele, will join the thousands of other writers in "the lumber of libraries" and the dustbin of the ages. Popularity is an index to popularity, and to nothing more.

Remarque's *All Quiet on the Western Front*, still popular, remains an effective enough anti-war tract, but it hardly competes with Hemingway's *A Farewell to Arms* or even with Norman Mailer's *The Naked and the Dead*. Though Remarque's style is terse and tense, his protagonist lacks significant personality or mind to be of lasting interest to the reader. Paul Bäumer doubtless was meant to be a kind of everyman, but he is as drab as he is desperate, and his yearnings are too commonplace to be interesting. Lew Ayres, placing Paul Bäumer in the American film version (1931), invested the character with more integrity and stubborn honor than Remarque had been able to suggest.

Remarque's novel is narrated by Bäumer in the first person. It is ironic that the book's most effective paragraphs are the final ones, in which Bäumer's voice ceases, and we are glad to receive a third-person narration though it be of the young man's death:

> He fell in October 1918, on a day that was so quiet and still on the whole front, that the army report confined itself to the single sentence: All quiet on the Western Front.
>
> He had fallen forward and lay on the earth as though sleeping. Turning him over one saw that he could not have suffered long; his face had an expression of calm, as though almost glad the end had come.

WILLIAM K. PFEILER

Remarque and Other Men of Feeling

Life at the Front is hard. It is hard for any man, even the big, hulking farmhands who have not a soft bone in their bodies, even on the city boys who are always ready for a scrap. But how much harder for the men who have learned to feel things deeply!

There is in Western culture a whole school of training which—unconsciously or not—centers upon sensibility. The artists and musicians and poets must feel deeply all things, life itself. For how can they create works of art without a mental acuteness of sensation? And if their whole training is to develop delicacy of mind and feeling, they certainly cannot have had a more inept preparation for life at the front!

Some of the best of war novels present the reaction of men of feeling to the war. They do not agree with one another, and naturally, for individual response is the essence of their training. Some are disappointing, and some reward the reader. Certain of them must be examined at length: Remarque's work, because of its fame, von der Vring's *Soldat Suhren*, because of its excellence, Wiechert's *Jedermann*, because it shows us a poet's behavior in the war, and Eisenlohr's work, because of its well-rounded picture of a selfish man.

Neither in length, scope, nor importance can the work of Erich Maria Remarque, whose novel, *Im Westen nichts Neues [All Quiet on the Western*

From *War and the German Mind: The Testimony of Men of Fiction Who Fought at the Front.* © 1941 Columbia University Press.

3

Front] (1928), became a world sensation, be compared to the epic achievement of Zweig. Its success will perhaps never be satisfactorily explained, but one fact seems certain: it cannot be due exclusively to extraordinary merit.

•Remarque is an artist. By his impressionistic talent he knows how to draw characters and situations that engage attention and arouse deepest sympathy. His language is versatile and concise; his narrative is rich in contrast of situations and reflections, and his composition is done with a brilliant stage technique. Lyric and idyllic scenes alternate with the most lurid and coarsest sort of realism. The intricate problems of life and of the War are cleverly reduced to such plain propositions that even the poorest in spirit can grasp them. Just at the most favorable psychological moment, when Zweig had broken the ice and the universal antiwar sentiment had reached its very climax, Remarque's story gave expression to the cry "No More War!"

But what are the facts and ideas of this book which claimed to tell of the fate of a whole generation?

A number of adolescents, college students, have been induced by their teacher to volunteer for war service. They and a few older men form a group somewhere at the Western Front. Their fate is the subject of the story, which was to be "neither an accusation nor a confession" but an attempt to give a report of "a generation that was destroyed by war, even though it might have escaped its shells." These pretensions of the author must be refuted. Ample evidence shows that the heroes of Remarque are not representative of a whole generation, but only of a certain type. This is not to criticize Remarque for military and other inconsistencies, but it is significant that in a book which claims to be a report of the front by a front soldier, of 288 pages of text only about 80 pages deal with situations at or right behind the front, and even they are heavily interspersed with reflections. Furthermore, it may be characteristic that the actual life at the front is described in general terms without ever a definite location given, while scenes behind the front, at hospitals, at home, in the barracks, etc., are given in a more clearly outlined realism. The implication is obvious; it leaves little doubt that many of his situations are fictitious.

What is more, the ethical character of the book provokes critical reflection. Through sordid detail and the description of gruesome and inhuman happenings, through reflection and innuendo, the condemnation of war amounts in the last analysis to a sweeping indictment of the older generation. It is as simple as that, and it would not evoke any criticism on our part, the guilt of the elders being a genuine problem, were it not for the superficial way in which Remarque goes about his task. Their teachers get the blame for the boys' being in a war which is of use "only to the Kaiser and the generals." With adolescent swagger, they call all culture "nonsense" [*Quatsch*] because they have to be out at the front, and when they have a chance they will pay their torturers back. For example, we find the hero on leave at home and looking at his books, among them all of the classical writers. He says: "I have read them with honest zeal, but most of them did not quite appeal to me; so much the more did I appreciate the other books, the more modern ones." This statement provides a good insight into the mind of the hero and his lack of appreciation for the values of the classical tradition. Again Lieutenant Mittelstedt "gets even" with his former teacher, now a drafted private. This particular scene, told with the malicious glee of an adolescent, is typical of the immature and sophomoric attitude of the heroes. So is the ever-recurring swagger and boastfulness of the young men who pose as old warriors well versed in all the tricks of warfare, though there is not one description of a feat actually executed, such as we find so abundantly and realistically in many other war books.

Individual incidents are given typical significance, less by an abstract process than by the exclusiveness with which they are presented. Thus the reader gets the impression that all officers are brutes; all teachers are cowardly shirkers who let others do the bloody and dangerous job of fighting for Germany's glory while they stay safely at home; and all doctors are inhuman monsters. Against this world of brutality are set off in shining lights the simple but genuine virtues of the common soldiers. They are all good fellows, and it arouses our sympathy to see them fall prey to power-drunk, sadistic superiors.

Immaturity and partiality by omission detract from the ethical import of this work which must be admitted to have force and human appeal. That the writer projects his 1927 mentality into the life of young World War soldiers is perhaps not so great a defect as is his wilfully narrowed outlook. *Im Westen nichts Neues* is scarcely a serious ethical document. Rather it is symptomatic of an age that saw the final revelation of the war in the adolescent self-pity, resentment, and sentimentality the novel embodies. Really it is the story of an egocentric, immature youngster of whom one may well wonder how he would have developed without the war. There is, indeed, plenty of authority for holding that the war helped many to find themselves and prove their mettle, and that it also exposed the brittle human substance that might have been broken by life anyway, without ever having been exposed to the destructive shells of war. It goes without saying that this observation—contradicting point-blank Remarque's claim to speak for a whole generation—implies neither that the war did not destroy the best of human values, nor that war was justifiable because it developed character.

Artistic powers of creation of Zweig's caliber are very rare. And they have even proved unnecessary in many a forceful war book. The reality of the war was so overpowering that a faithful account of it often found its own adequate form; that is to say, the subject matter made the writer. This can be seen in the failures of many sequels to war novels. Few of the war writers produced more than one successful novel. One of these rare exceptions is George von der Vring, whose book *Soldat Suhren* [*Private Suhren*] (1927) is a novel of finest artistic and human quality. Here again is the story of a group of men who are trained for and put into the mill of the war; here, too, we see the common scenes and incidents of the soldier's life. If we consider artistic composition, however, and seriousness of judgment, *Suhren* justifies a position of its own.

The title reflects the individualism and the humility of heart prevailing in this story. The experience of a young artist, a painter, and his closer comrades, their progress from their first uncertain steps as recruits to their first battle, is told with directness and restraint but intense sympathy. The reality of external details is well balanced by revelations of the inner life; and these are reserved and given with pathos, humor, and lyric quality. Von der Vring is a master in creating atmosphere, in conjuring moods and aesthetic effects, but he is also an honest reporter of the ugly aspects of war which he sees always with the trained eyes of the artist.

Private Suhren is an individualist and remains one, for the meaning of his being herded off to war does not become very clear to him, and he does not see himself fully as a part of a common destiny. But if in his heart he stays aloof from his fellow men, this attitude has nothing defined about it. His reserve is the natural result of uncompromising intellectual honesty and a deep feeling of responsibility toward his destiny as a human being and an artist. He has no delusions about himself; he is not an eagle, as he would like to be, but neither is he a domestic chicken. Rather he compares himself with a partridge, that likes to live its life in freedom. Although he could well have escaped service through malingery skillfully executed, he continues in a service of self-effacement. It makes him happy, after all, since he feels it the honorable thing to do, even though the meaning of his duty remains obscure. He loves the fatherland and his home town, in memory of which he writes a most charming lyrical poem, but he also realizes that God created all nations. The nations are like the petals of a flower painted by an artist; they gleam around God in a single beautiful color. Similarity and an equal claim to life and light is the essence of the petals; and so it is also of the peoples. There are slight variations, certainly, yet it is the equality which makes the wonderful flower we call mankind. It is clear to Suhren that the front against the enemies of Germany is confusing. Good fights against good, evil against evil, good against evil, and evil against good. It is a front deranged and perverted a thousand ways that the men are fighting on, and nobody can make out its final form. But one front does exist, which is clear, simple, and straight, hidden deep in a secret place, in the conscience itself. It is the front of kind thoughts and deeds of human worth, of clasped hands and loyal faith.

In the crushing experiences of his environment he finds refuge in his dreams, dreams of human and artistic substance, of love, childhood memories, and art, dreams which do not enervate but strengthen. The superiority—under the stress of the reality of war—of these elements of Suhren's strong and simple faith over philosophies and conventional religion is well pointed out.

Suhren's individualism is not determined by an inflated ego, but by a sense of responsibility vis-à-vis a system which denied in its representatives the principles of a true community. Later works of von der Vring show a consistently developed approach toward a true spirit of community. They reveal much more of an ethnocentric character, and need not be regarded as contradictions to Suhren; rather they indicate Suhren's natural evolution.

Von der Vring presented the war through the eyes of an artist whose outstanding qualities were honest simplicity, lyrical charm, and unpretentious human sympathy. Suhren moves in a class of people among whom the leading elements are teachers in grade schools. The circle of the artist hero of Ernst Wiechert's *Jedermann* [Everyman] (1931) is of quite a different sort.

Johannes is a law student, but he can live only the creative life of a poet. The nailed boots of soldiers seem to him to trample into the dirt the individual qualities of life and of the spirit, so much that not even the name of a man remains. The soul becomes a figure, an entity for which only the indefinite personal pronoun "one" is justified. His whole life has prepared him to keep from giving himself over to collective concerns that demand subordination and devotion to a passion that has its origin in the mass of men and its character determined thereby. He can only mistrust everything in the line of tradition, school, teachers, authorities, and he hates to be *eingesetzt* "inserted," like a letter of type which attains meaning and significance only through combination with others. All purpose in the life of an individual is extinguished by war because one fate awaits everyone: exhaustion and senseless, lawless dying, that begins long before actual death terminates a wretched existence.

Despite his utter unfitness for war, Johannes stands up to the duty he assumed when he volunteered. But unlike von der Vring's Suhren, who generated out of his own individual resources the decision for a responsible active participation in war, Johannes needs and receives powerful aid from the outside to see him through.

There are first the friends in his group who help him. Count Percy's unfailing and self-assured conduct, bred in him in a fixed, aristocratic world, challenges Johannes to match these qualities with the forces provided by the aristocracy of the spirit. His dejected and weak friend Klaus, like Percy a former schoolmate, arouses in him deep and genuine sympathy, which, leading to a true helpfulness in spirit and deed, also benefits the helper. And then there is Comrade Oberüber, the homeless vagabond, whose common sense and earthiness serve as a wholesome corrective for the dangerous over-sensibility of the poet.

But the real strength comes from the Eternal Feminine. To his mother and his love he owes endurance, sanity, honor, and a faith in the ultimate meaning of life. He learns that it is for his mother when he fights in the war, and if he dies in action, it will be for her. The mother becomes to him a symbol into which merge all the forces of life eternal; indeed, elements of the "Oedipus complex" are also in evidence, and play a part throughout the story.

With these supports Johannes finds he is able to save the remnants of his real self from the war, which otherwise means emptiness of heart and abandonment of all thinking, a war that is an endless road in storm and rain, an eternal waiting, a wasting of all values, and above all, the loss of the self.

Wiechert is bitterly abusive towards war, for example, "Whenever death feels hungry, then we are sold to him like bread, which he digests to dung." But he recognizes other than egocentric values as parts of the defensive mechanism of the individual; thus, it is the feeling of being one with his column that shelters the lost soul.

The justification for Wiechert's attitude of positive individualism is that the artist or poet as an individual creating for all humanity should have nothing to do with war, any more than mothers, the eternal bearers of life.

A definite weakness of the book is the number of unexplained allusions to experiences in the pre-war lives of the characters. It is chiefly on account of these that Wiechert fails to make the story a more satisfactory literary achievement. Indeed, the advantages of outlining in more detail the pre-war lives of the men depicted at the front are so apparent that it is surprising that this has been done in the German war novel so seldom. It certainly would have lent depth of focus to many stories. Among the few books that lead a character from a typical pre-war setting into and through the war is the novel of Friedrich Eisenlohr, *Das gläserne Netz* [*The Net of Glass*] (1927). Here the egocentric attitude shows no responsibility toward a creative task or mission; rather it is a crude and unscrupulous egotism, made unpalatable by the camouflage of a high-sounding "new" morality. The book depicts a certain pre-war type of impressionistic man and his conduct in war, seven hundred pages of reflections and deeds of a rather unimportant, if representative, ego.

Arthur, the son of a high German official, is still a student. After having often changed his mind about his future profession, he breaks with his father and goes to the free atmosphere of Paris to develop his talents in his own fashion. On a trip to Germany he is caught by the outbreak of the war and must serve in the army, where he soon becomes a lieutenant, due to previous training and social position. Slightly wounded in the beginning, he hastens away from the front. Through clever and consistent malingering he removes himself from the combat zone for the rest of the war. He occupies comfortable and remunerative posts in the rear, where he can in safety "develop his higher personality." Numerous erotic adventures help in his education. He averts the occasional danger of being called back to the front by ruthless blackmailing methods. Thus, to the influential father of his former fiancée he reveals and threatens to publicize the intimacies he has had with her. Again he subtly hints about his knowledge of his superior's addiction to morphine. Having large war pay, he lives in luxury with his mistress, rejecting bribes of harassed Belgians only because they would put him under obligation to the despised plebs. Meanwhile his mother is growing weaker and weaker from lack of food. She dies. And in the end, after all these years of self-indulgence, he faces the future with pompous words of maturity and resolution.

This gentleman, who has brought misery and grief to many people, regards himself and his welfare as important out of all proportion to the rights of his fellow men. Consequently much of his argumentation about ethical and social problems sounds hollow. He will not give up the claim to individuality for the sake of the "superstition of ideals of community" and authority, which have their roots in romantic subordination. Only supreme, courageous loyalty to oneself gives back to life its true color and fertility; hence no heed should be paid to the civilization of modern society, that patina of cowardice, stupor, poverty, and brutality.

Through a world catastrophe, a proletarian revolution, salvation will come for sexual, public, and private ills. One may seem to drift aimlessly from adventure to adventure, but the only meaningful existence is to wait for this catastrophe. When it comes, a newer and truer life will be built on the foundation of unbiased personal freedom and individual responsibility. The state, whose very basis he rejects, has no right to throw men into the witches' cauldron of war without first giving aims, ideas, and faith that stand up against individual skepticism. Nothing and nobody can do good to the mass as a collective being. Only the individual can help himself by shaking off each and every authority, for authority exists only by falsifying human reality in terms of romantic idealism. Moral scruples must be resolutely left behind as bourgeois atavism, and the result will be a sublimated individuality on the basis of natural and eternal laws. Only the anarchists can be truly international, because they occupy themselves exclusively with themselves.

The ethics of this individual and his conduct in war are perfectly congruent. The egocentric attitude per se has found an extreme and presumptuous formulation. The hero is an isolated, atomistic individual and remains one, and many of his theories are more the outgrowth of his selfish character than the results of insight and logical conclusions.

Self-preservation is natural, and no moral stigma is attached to it. Man recoils from the horror of war and tries desperately to save himself. The varied ways he follows for this purpose can be readily appreciated, yet the cloaking of crass egotism with a mantle of a higher ethics is painful and embarrassing. Eisenlohr has succeeded well in presenting the development before and during the war of an intellectual and moral snob who does this. Fortunately, this sort of inflated moralizing is not very frequent.

EDWIN M. MOSELEY

Christ As Doomed Youth:
Remarque's All Quiet on the Western Front

D. H. Lawrence's deification of the physical succeeded in shocking the orthodox thinkers of his time, and he was not averse to calling the world's attention to the fact that it should be shocked. In his famous essay on "Pornography and Obscenity," he had a passing word of praise for the amorality of post-World War I youth and a lengthy verbal spanking for the Victorians, who to his way of thinking had made sex filthy. One doubts if the youngsters who were so conscious of being "lost" could approach coitus as a "baptism of fire" any more than Miriam could—or more to the point here, the unintellectual Clara.

Lawrence's making a religion of the physical is a paradoxical development of the naturalistic tradition in fiction. In sense, poor Emma Bovary asked no more or less than Paul Morel, and Flaubert effectively pointed out that she was questing death under the verbal guise of life, freedom, and transcendent love. The trouble may be that Emma imitated the artists without the capacity to be an artist; she was not sufficiently a stranger to life to find in life more than the prosaic. Like Paul, she tended to talk about "God in everything," but unlike Paul, she did not feel it.

What would Conrad and Dostoyevsky and Turgenev have said about Lawrence's brand of mysticism? When Lawrence's Christ experienced in his loins, "I am risen!" would Conrad have said, "the liver, not the soul"? The

From *Pseudonyms of Christ in the Modern Novel: Motifs and Methods.* © 1962 by the University of Pittsburgh.

old question of where the seat of the soul is, comes up: in the brain, in the heart, between the legs, or the indefinable "something else besides" located, to be sure, everywhere and nowhere? Perhaps it is a matter of tone—my gross "between the legs" is hardly Lawrence's "magnificent, blazing indomitable in the depths of his loins." Conrad may have accepted the reverence in Lawrence's attitude despite the extreme physicality of his imagery and, indeed, theme. Miriam and Sonia are both like burning white lights, but Dostoyevsky's drama moves us toward Sonia and Lawrence's away from Miriam. Lawrence in effect invalidates the orthodox dualistic approach to man, for in him the body is the end *and* the beginning. It is hardly the nature of man for which penance must be done.

Lawrence's immersion in the physical, as we have suggested, is an ironic outgrowth of the nihilistic naturalism of which Bazarov, for example, was guilty. According to the tone of Turgenev, the naturalistic, deterministic, monistic climate of the nineteenth century was pathetic by its very nature. He accused it of having forgotten the eternal verities validated by the truth of experience, not by the testings of science. In this same naturalistic climate Lawrence somehow found these verities. As much as it was the Victorians, was it the naturalistic writers themselves—Flaubert, Zola, Norris, Dreiser— who presented man's very physicality as his pathetic plight? Lawrence would not have it so: contrast the tone implicit, say, in Epstein's famous statue of Adam with, again, Lawrence's "I am risen!"

Most of the writers of the first two decades of this century were concerned more with man's imprisonment in a social cage rather than in the cage of the flesh. If the latter to Lawrence was no cage at all, the former was frequently implicit in the enveloping action which he created for his characters. The Marxist critic, we have seen, tended to make the social pathos all important in the early Lawrence, but actually such emphasis was never major in his works. Lawrence's Christ, when he was young, had a reforming zeal to save the world, but the concern with the public mission was defined as death itself. *The Man Who Died* can be read on one level as Lawrence's saying to his contemporaries that social consciousness is part of a *mock*-quest. Dostoyevsky would have agreed on that much, but the point of body-consciousness at which Lawrence arrived he might have restated as the irreligious, physical hedonism of his satanic Svidrigailov.

The pathos of the naturalistic approach, from which Lawrence's worship of the body ironically freed him, was accentuated for the slightly younger writers by the experience of World War I. The poetry of Wilfred Owen, the remarkably talented young Englishman who died in France in 1918, a week before the Armistice, contained within its few lines most of the attitudes which the post-war novelists were to express in recollection.

He contrasted the reality of death to the illusions of the society at home: if you could see war, he told the generation which had reared and educated him,

> you would not tell with such high zest
> To children ardent for some desperate glory,
> The old lie: *Dulce et decorum est*
> *Pro patria mori.*

He pointed up the ironies of youth caught in a plight it did not make and did not understand. "What passing-bells for these who die as cattle?" He asked rhetorically, but proceeded to give an answer that inverted traditional religious imagery and reduced it to a mockery:

> Only the monstrous anger of the guns.
> Only the stuttering rifles' rapid rattle
> Can patter out their hasty orisons.

The attack on the lies by which we live, the comparison of men to trapped animals, the ironic juxtaposition of the words of resurrection and the experience of final death were all characteristic of the nineteenth-century naturalism which so disturbed Dostoyevsky, Turgenev, and Conrad. Furthermore, they continued to be characteristic of the new writing well through the 1920's.

Still, something about the tone and mood of Owen was not completely without hope and consolation, and this elusive positiveness sometimes breaks through the pathos and dominates the poetry. It was inevitable that writers compared young men dying in war to Christ as the crucified innocent, and Owen repeatedly did so directly and implicitly. In some poems, the tone was anger at the crucifiers (not the enemy, but the older generation of one's own parents and leaders), and these were without consolation in the face of death. But in other poems, though the world was rejected as lost morally and the young soldiers described as lost physically, there is a groping to express the transcendent beauty of the untouched innocents on the battlefield.

> Heart, you were never hot,
> Nor large, nor full like hearts made great with shot;
> And though your hand be pale,
> Paler are all which trail
> Your cross through flame and hail:
> Weep, you may weep, for you may touch them not.

Or in still another poem, a Christ-like figure met in a dream identifies himself:

> I am the enemy you killed, my friend,

and forgivingly accepts his murderers into the company of those who, when the time comes, will rise to cleanse the chariot wheels of the world of the blood which will clog them till they can no longer turn. In a final version of this poem, the Christ-figure speaks to the young soldier:

> Beauty is yours and you have mastery,
> Wisdom is mine, and I have mystery.

An aura of tenderness and belief is in constant conflict with anger and pathetic resignation. The latter, again, is frequently revealed through mock-religious imagery and the former through the serious use of Christ as a correlative.

Remarque's *All Quiet on the Western Front*, completed ten years after Owen's death, achieves a similar paradox of softness in the midst of harshness. In this sense it is strikingly different from the number of war novels that are basically stories of the development of youth from naïve commitment to experienced detachment. Hemingway's *A Farewell to Arms*, a great novel on many levels, is an example of the initiation story in which the innocent in the modern world learns that he is vulnerable to hurt by an indifferent universe and that the length of his survival depends on deliberate protection against vulnerability. To be sure, Hemingway's characters are always questing love, a home, religion, order, but they do not find them because they are unwilling to admit that suffering and sacrifice are essential to achieved commitment. The structure of the book is tight: a step by step journey from innocence to experience. And the style is economic in keeping with the theme of the advisability of hiding the emotions from a world which will torture them.

All Quiet makes basically the same points as *A Farewell to Arms*, but its methods are totally unlike Hemingway's and its mood is different. Remarque's constant refrain is literally: "We are a lost generation," we who were too young to have roots in experience and who have discovered that the words intended as roots by parents, teachers, preachers, politicians have no relationship to experience. Remarque's hero is nineteen when the book begins and twenty when he dies, and he has a strong feeling that even the men of twenty-five who have wives and children of their own have a sense of something to return to. In one scene the soldiers typically discuss what they will do when the peace comes, but with a sense that the young men dragged out of school into war have had no chance even to create the lies by which men live in peacetime. Now, facing the truth of death so soon, they are denied the years of illusion which are the luxury of living before every man faces the heart of darkness and makes his individual adjustment to it.

Remarque's protagonist Paul, who tells his own story, is constantly surprised that at the age of nineteen he has, as Hemingway might put it, "lived with death a long time." According to Paul, his journey of learning was practically completed in his "first bombardment." In that moment, "the world as they [the older generation] taught it to us broke in pieces . . . we saw that there was nothing of their world left. We were all at once terribly alone; and alone we must see it through." For the archetypal sacrificial heroes, death and the aloneness with which one faces it come at the end of the epic drama, but Paul in effect begins with them. This consciousness of the shocking shortening of the journey of learning is forever with us in the novel. It is in every episode, and it is in image after image. In a day a child moves from innocence to experience. In a year a young man moves from maturity to death. At the climax of the novel Paul moves across a foxhole to a French soldier whom he has killed because he had to:

> I drag myself toward him, hesitate, support myself on my hands, creep a bit farther, wait, again a terrible journey of three yards, a long, a terrible journey.

This is the most telling image of the book, "a terrible journey of three yards," a life shortened in space as throughout the novel it is shortened in time.

Here is indeed the essence of art. Selection, the symbolic short cut, careful manipulation of structure allow us to live a lifetime in two hours in the theater or through thirty pages or a thousand in fiction. It is literally time and space that are shortened for us so that we suspend our disbelief and accept the eternal and the universal which endure beyond all time and space. In these terms, Greek tragedy is perhaps the epitome of art in that it juxtaposes the vastest of themes with the greatest limitations of time and space. There is something here subtly akin to the essential pun that we mentioned before: timelessness is effectively proclaimed in a short time! At the beginning of the play, Oedipus seems to be on two feet. The attaining of his lofty position even from birth is traced for us in summary after summary: the very technique of the delved-out memory is essential to the central narrative. Before the day is done Oedipus has moved from innocence and pride to experience and humility. He leaves the stage virile and kingly in appearance, though aged now in spirit, and returns suddenly and shockingly a broken old man, the guise of the flesh compatible with the state of the soul. As if this were not enough, now old, he is for the first time truly young; now blind, he at last sees. All of this literally artistically in less than an hour!

But the overall method of Remarque that reflects his dominant image of the journey of life in an infinitesimal context of space and time is more romantic than classical. The classical writer tells a story clearly and surely step by step, from exposition through separable steps of the complication up to a climax and into a denouement. He creates a readily outlined narrative, reducing the overwhelmingly general to the excruciatingly sharp specific. He creates drama in the traditional sense of the word: ideas and judgments are implicit in the overt action of his characters. Let us put it this way: the method of the classicist is logical and chronological though his theme may be the irrationality of rational man and the absurdity of time. On the other hand, the romantic story-teller has constantly groped for a method that has a less ironic and a more literal relationship to the emotional nature of man and the smallness of time and space. Sterne, Proust, Joyce, Virginia Woolf have all tried to free their stories of man from order as indeed, to their way of thinking, man is truly freed from it. Their methods are associative rather than chronological. Another way of putting it: more lyric than narrative, more poetic than prose-like.

All Quiet achieves its disregard of time through a kind of lyric method. Paul, the protagonist, tells his story in an almost impressionistic manner. He moves back and froth in time from the present moment to past moments as details of the present suggest episodes of the past to him. He moves between the description of action and the lyrical expression of feelings and evaluations. The events that evolve *can* be placed in time and space, but this is not important: the effect is lyrical and tender, not epic and grand, the emotional expression of a moment to which a lifetime has been reduced. In structure, as in that of so many first novels, *All Quiet* seems loose, unpolished, youthful, but it *is* youthful and therein is both its failure and its success as art.

In one passage of the kind of lyricism to which I refer, Paul is speaking:

> It is chilly. I am on sentry and stare into the darkness. My strength is exhausted as always after an attack, and so it is hard for me to be alone with my thoughts. They are not properly thoughts; they are memories which in my weakness turn homeward and strangely move me.
>
> The parachute-lights shoot upwards—and I see a picture, a summer evening. I am in a cathedral cloister and look at the tall rose trees that bloom in the middle of the little cloister garden where the monks lie buried. Around the walls are the stone

carvings of the Stations of the Cross. No one is there. A great quietness rules in this blossoming quadrangle, the sun lies warm on the heavy grey stones. I place my hand upon them and feel the warmth. At the right-hand corner the green cathedral spire ascends into the pale blue sky of the evening. Between the glowing columns of the cloister is the cool darkness that only churches have, and I stand there and wonder whether, when I am twenty, I shall have experienced the bewildering emotions of love.

The image is alarmingly near; it touches me before it dissolves in the light of the next star-shell.

The Stations of the Cross is a correlative to which the reader responds intuitively, and I respond to it deliberately as well in terms of the Christ-motif in which I have been interested. For the moment, follow these responses, the intuitive and deliberate one, and see where they lead us. When we come across the direct reference to Christ, we think with a feeling akin to *pieta* of the plight of Paul and the other young men being sacrificed in the war. We may think too of the young men bearing the cross for an entire society which with good or bad intentions has condemned them to die. We think, in this passage at least, of death as a way to life, for the imagery of the passage is that of growth and regeneration: rose trees blooming in the night, a "blossoming quadrangle" of stone still warm with the day's sun, a green spire reaching upward into a blue sky. Or we may think on the other hand of a kind of lost Eden for which Paul longs in world of death. In the paragraph which follows, Paul himself describes the memory as a "calm" one, but a calmness against which he must protect himself lest he drop his defenses against the everlasting "unquietness" of the front.

Or more deliberately: The Stations of the Cross which Paul recalls having seen in a cathedral garden were the pictorial representations, sometimes in painting, sometimes as here in bas-relief, of Christ's "journey" from his condemnation to death up to the point at which his body was laid in the tomb. Church lore differs as to how many "stations" there actually were, but most representations suggest the following fourteen: (1) Christ is condemned to death; (2) the cross is laid upon him; (3) he falls for the first time; (4) he meets his Blessed Mother; (5) Simon of Cyrene is made to bear the cross; (6) Christ's face is wiped by Veronica; (7) he falls for the second time; (8) he meets the women of Jerusalem; (9) he falls for the the third time; (10) he is stripped of his garments; (11) he is crucified; (12) he dies on the cross; (13) his body is taken down from the cross; (14) his body is laid in the tomb. In the Middle Ages a definite ritual developed around these picturizations whereby the devotee went in effect on a miniature vicarious pilgrimage along the way Christ traversed in Jerusalem from Pilate's house to Mount Calvary. The more fortunate devout of course actually made the trip to Jerusalem and traversed in person the "Via Dolorosa," as the way of the cross became known.

Remarque's reader soon thinks of the way of the cross again, for on the very next page Paul says that the way of those who have roots is the way of nostalgia, but for himself and the other lost ones, "these memories of former times do not awaken desire so much as sorrow—a strange, apprehensible melancholy." The way of his generation, like the way of Christ bearing the cross, *is* the way of sorrow. The very imagery of the journey is with us once more:

> Today we could pass through the scenes of our youth like travellers. . . . We long to be there; but could we live there?
> We are forlorn like children, and experienced like old men, we are crude and sorrowful and superficial—I believe we are lost.

Paul's journey, then, like Christ's, is the "via dolorosa," the way from the condemnation to death, to the actual death on the last page of the novel. This is not as far as we can deliberately go with the image, the Stations of the Cross. It would be an interesting piece of craftsmanship if, say, the steps of Paul's journey to his death were symbolically those of Christ, in the same way that the twelve central adventures of Joyce's Stephen follow the divisions of the *Odyssey*, but in this book Remarque is not that kind of a writer. Having taken the Stations of the Cross as a correlative, one might relate the gambling for Christ's garments to Remarque's motif of: Who will get the dead man's shoes? The removing of the shoes from the dying is an age-old folk motif that can be read on as many levels as, say, Oedipus, and in some versions its implications are not unlike those of the soldiers' desiring Christ's robe without respect for his death. But in *All Quiet* the claiming of the clothes of the dead men is not part of any structure analogous to the traditional structure of Christ's Stations. Remarque's structure, as we have said, is more lyrical and associative than narrative and logical.

The Stations of the Cross, then, is a dominant image at a pivotal point, but neither a key to overall structure nor a part of any cluster of images more specific than the broad sacrificial-hero ones. We have mentioned before a possible difference between integrated meanings and parallel ones. The difference is not always valid, but pursuit of the parallel as if it were an integral part of the whole quickly points up the precariously parasitic and absurd nature of literary criticism. I admit my own tendency toward critical venturing. In the light of my own interest in the Christ patterns of the novels in which I had at first *intuitively* discovered them, I *did* look up Stations of the Cross. The sources which I read with interest listed the "stations" or steps in Christ's final journey to death in much the same way as I have above and besides discussed the derivation of the word *station*. A *station*, according to one source, is a fast of bread and water, whereby as pilgrims we simulate the suffering of Christ. Even in this sense, it may come from a military metaphor that occurs several times in the Bible as, for example, in ". . . we are also God's soldiers," the Latin word for soldier or military guard having been *statio*. Ah, I said, *station . . . soldier . . . also God's soldiers . . .* Remarque's soldier Paul. Another source referred station more directly to *stationarius*, "a military encampment," and then figuratively, "an encampment protecting one from the assaults of the devil." Again, *station . . .* the place in which we *stand* to repel the enemy . . . the manifold irony that the word *enemy* has taken on by Remarque's last page. True, creative writing demands creative reading, but the obligation of the reader is to be imaginative *within* the limits of the book. Parallels are interesting and enlightening, but pursuing them is like playing a game for which there are no rules: it's both too easy and too hard.

One is tempted to play a similar game with the name Paul. In *Sons and Lovers*, for example, where some of the names are obviously symbolic, the protagonist Paul is called by his intimates "'Postle," teasing the reader to consider the associations of the Biblical name. The Biblical Paul was martyred for his letters. He felt himself free of the conventional law, for the true law was in the mystic union of the believer with the crucified Lord. He emphasized the purity of family life. He preached fellowship not only with Christ but with fellow-believers. Is Lawrence pointing to any one of these associations, or all of them, or none? Does an awareness of the apostle Paul's literary martyrdom enrich Lawrence's motif of the artist and the society? Perhaps this much at least. And what of Remarque's Paul? Does an awareness of the Biblical Paul's preaching of fellowship enrich young Paul's refrain that the "finest thing that arose out of the war" was "comradeship"? Coincidentally and significantly, yes, but hardly because Remarque was using the name Paul as a guide to meaning.

Comradeship in the face of death is essentially a religious idea, and Remarque handles it as such throughout his novel. Communion as a kind of holy eating together by way of transcending the death to which men are damned is a dominant image of the book. There is a wonderful scene in which Paul and Kat, the older man who serves as a kind of natural mentor to Paul and his group, eat a goose they have stolen in a previous comic episode. They eat, and two men who "formerly . . . should not have had a single thought in common . . . sit with a goose between us and feel in unison, and are so intimate that we do not even speak. . . . I love him. . . . We are brothers and press on one another the choicest pieces." Later, in a deserted village to which Paul, Kat, and others are assigned, there is a long, happy last eating scene before Paul is wounded. In the last narrative action of the book Paul carries the wounded Kat back to the post. On the way Paul thinks that Kat has fainted, but when he arrives, he discovers that his burden has been hit in the head with a splinter. Paul has saved Kat only to have him die. An orderly, noticing Paul's stunned response, asks: "You are not related, are you?" "No, we are not related. No, we are not related," Paul thinks with all of the ironic awareness that every man is related to every other man. This Paul like the other one preached fellowship with those in the same plight with himself.

If all men are brothers, who then is the enemy? Paul looks at Russian prisoners through a barbed wire fence. He knows that the very "word of command" which has made them enemies can transform them into friends. He is frightened, for to think in that way lies "the abyss." If he is to survive, he must repress these thoughts until after the war has ended. Then, perhaps, pursuing them, he might give purpose to his questless life. Paul breaks his cigarettes in half and shares them with the Russians; he gives them part of the cakes his mother has made for him.

The scene with the Russians is preparation for the climax of the book which we have already mentioned in another connection. Paul, lost from his patrol, is hiding in a fox hole. He stabs a retreating Frenchman who falls into the hole beside him. Watching him die, Paul at last makes the "terrible journey" of three yards across the bottom of the hole till he is beside his victim. By three o'clock the man is dead. After all, Paul's maturation turns out not to have been completed in that first bombardment. Never before has he seen a man die whom he, Paul, has killed with his own hands. Throughout the book Paul and his friends have blamed worldwide diplomats, the Kaiser, the generals, the manufacturers, the parents, the preachers, the teachers for their plight in the war, but now Paul takes responsibility for the sins of man in which he has participated. "Forgive me, comrade; how could you be my enemy? If we threw away these rifles and this uniform you could be my brother just like Kat." Paul swears a life of penance and sacrifice for the death of the man whose life has been bound up in some mysterious way with his own life. He promises to devote himself after the war to helping his "enemy's" family. He has crucified a stranger, and he *will* suffer for this greatest of all sins.

But back in the trenches with his own men, he is reassured and comforted. "After all, war is war." Business is business, and life is life. This is the conscious world where the devil rules. To deny it, that is, to pursue the godhead, is martyrdom on behalf of one's brothers. That way lies "the abyss," according to convention and the devil. But according to the godhead which

Paul would imitate if he could, that way is salvation. What Paul learns in his journey for a moment and for all time is that man cannot pursue the truth and live. Of course, as Hemingway says, if he does not pursue it, he dies too, but only a little later. The joker is that the early death in the cause of truth may be the one way to the everlasting life.

HELMUT LIEDLOFF

Two War Novels: A Critical Comparison

Hemingway's *A Farewell to Arms* and Remarque's *Im Westen nichts Neues* are two of the few books about World War I which are still read today, which have the reputation of being classics in this field. In the case of *Farewell* it would be belabouring the obvious to prove the general critical acclaim. In the case of *Im Westen* the case appears to be less clear. To some post-World-War-Two critics it is "only" a report, journalistically written, not of sufficient depth, in short: not serious literature. Wilhelm Duwe, however, claims it is written "mit einer Anschaulichkeit, die in der gesamten Kriegsliteratur nicht ihresgleichen hat." Harvey Swados agrees with this positive note when, in a very recent article, he says: "Surely no one can read it [*All Quiet on the Western Front*] without that immediate quickening which in itself is sufficient to intimate that one holds in one's hands an imperishable work." Swados is quite specific in pointing out the artistic merit of the novel when he says:

> It does not follow however that *All Quiet* is an artless work. It is at least as difficult to be simple and direct as to be convoluted and subtle when dealing with the brutalizing effects of continuous terror and sudden death, for sentimentalizing is as difficult to avoid on the one hand as obscurantism on the other.

From *Revue de Littérature comparée*. © 1968 Centre National de la Recherche Scientifique.

This author agrees with Duwe and Swados. His opinion is furthermore supported by the tremendous success *Im Westen* has had over the years; it has been, in fact, one of the most successful German novels of this century. Within eighteen months after publication three and one-half million copies were sold and it was translated into twenty-five languages. By 1951 six million copies had been sold.

The similarity of the topics invites a critical comparison of the two novels in regard to symbolism, language, structure, development of character, the extent of the depiction of war, and the attitude of the authors towards war. It should be pointed out, though, that Hemingway has engaged the attention of critics much more than Remarque. This circumstance heavily influences the emphasis on Remarque in this paper.

Right in the beginning of the two novels, one of the main differences between them becomes obvious. Many critics have noted that the opening of *Farewell* expresses in its symbolism almost the entire story: the clearness, the dryness, the leaves falling early that year, the richness of the crops, and, finally, the rain. These symbols appear again and again throughout the novel, e.g. the rain as a leitmotif suggesting death. There is little doubt that *Farewell* makes extensive use of symbolism, whereas *Im Westen* employs comparatively little. Some instances in the latter, however, appear as a definite attempt in this direction. For instance, when Paul comes home from the front, he finds that his suit fits no more, suggesting that he outgrew his past and everything he left when he became a soldier. Among other things, he left his butterfly collection, which is mentioned twice. Taken together with the fluttering butterflies which rest on the teeth of the skull before the front trench they might be understood as suggesting the world of beauty that Paul has to leave behind. The movie made use of the butterfly in this sense at the very end: on a quiet day, when Paul is in the front trench, a butterfly flutters near before him. Paul forgets for a minute his by then almost instinctive cautiousness, reaches for the butterfly and is hit at that very moment by a sniper's bullet. His latent yearning for the world of beauty is finally fatal. Paul's last name is suggestive of this yearning for beauty, as the name Bäumer brings to mind both "Baum" (tree) and "Träumer" (dreamer), two terms which have considerable significance for Paul's character. Tree suggests organic growth, the idea of wholeness—things Paul is yearning for or dreaming of. Some other names also have a suggestive quality. Thus the name Haie Westhus has a regional form and points to Haie's close relation to his moor, while the name of Katcinsky, which has in it the word for "cat," points in another direction. As the head of the group, he is "zäh, schlau, gerissen, . . . und [mit] einer wunderbaren Witterung für dicke Luft, gutes Essen und schöne

Druckposten," all qualities which make us think of the instinct of an animal. In a later paragraph the importance of the animal image will be discussed.

Although the importance of symbolism in *Farewell* is obvious, a comparative analysis of both novels suggests that it should not be carried too far, either. One critic, for instance, by applying too rigid a symbolic framework, sees the Rinaldi of after the "bad summer" as a man without resources, without God, as a man of the plain. This interpretation disregards other details of the story, e.g., that Rinaldi belongs to the group, that he is a close friend of Frederic, and that his partial breakdown occurs after the "bad summer" precisely because he is very much aware of what is going on, because he is "realizing" the war. Remarque is much more explicit on the topic of the breakdown than Hemingway. When the group returns from visiting the dying Kemmerich, it happens to Kropp:

> Plötzlich wirft der kleine Kropp seine Zigarette weg, trampelt wild darauf herum, sieht sich um, mit einem aufgelösten und verstörten Gesicht und stammelt: "Verfluchte Scheisse, diese verfluchte Scheisse."

This case of "Frontkoller," as Remarque calls it, reminds one very much of that of Rinaldi after the "bad summer." He unreasonably attacks the priest:

> "To hell with you, priest!" . . . "To hell with you," said Rinaldi. "To hell with the whole damn business." He sat back in his chair . . . "I don't give a damn," Rinaldi said to the table. "To hell with the whole business." He looked defiantly around the table, his eyes flat, his face pale.

Remarque records two other cases of seasoned soldiers suddenly breaking down: Detering, who deserts and is caught shortly thereafter and shot, and Berger, who forgets his usually instinctive caution to take care of a wounded dog and gets fatally hurt. To speak of these men as being "without resources," to put them into one category with the unaware, the incompetent, does not seem justified.

Through the same emphasis on the supposedly basic symbolic structure of the novel, the figure of the priest and the cold, clear mountain world are made the antithesis of the filthy, godless plain where the war is fought. However, fighting and rain do occur in the mountains, too, and the love story does take place in Milan, a city of the plain. Interestingly enough, also in *Im Westen* there appears a series of paragraphs describing a much-longed-for, wholesome world. Two of them may serve as examples:

Flache Wiesen, Felder, Höfe—ein Gespann zieht einsam vor dem Himmel über den Weg, der parallel zum Horizon läuft. Eine Schranke, vor der Bauern warten, Mädchen, die winken, Kinder, die am Bahndamm spielen, Wege, die ins Land führen, glatte Wege, ohne Artillerie.

. . . die Wälder mit ihren Birkenrändern. Sie wechseln jeden Augenblick die Farbe. Jetzt leuchten die Stämme im hellsten Weiss, und seidig und luftig schwebt zwischen ihnen das pastellhafte Grün des Laubes;—im nächsten Moment wechselt alles zu einem opalenen Blau, das silbrig vom Rande her streicht und das Grün forttuptf; . . .

The beauty and wholesomeness of this "other" world is recognized in either case. But both Bäumer and Lt. Henry realize that they are not part of it. This becomes particularly clear if one carefully reads the description of the Abbruzzi by the priest; it is not a real possibility for Henry—it is an idyll, and so is the life with Catherine in the Alps above Montreux idyllic. Reality, the war, death, the rain will catch up with them.

Parallel to the greater importance of symbols in Hemingway is the greater restraint in his language. His adjectives and verbs are strictly descriptive, with very little directly emotional value. For instance the scene at the bridge where Lt. Henry is arrested: nowhere is there any of his feeling given, everything is transposed into situation and action:

The other one grabbed me from behind and pulled my arm up so that it twisted in the socket. I turned with him and the other one grabbed me around the neck. I kicked his shins and got my left knee into his groin.

Another good example is Frederic's farewell from Catherine in Milan or the closing paragraph of the novel. The detachment, which is not necessarily an inner one, is stressed by the frequent use of the "there are" phrase and such words as "nice, lovely, fine" etc. These worn-out words with almost no precise meaning at all contribute to the low-key atmosphere of the whole.

Although both novels are told in the first person—how different is Remarque's language. Colloquialisms occur not only in the dialogue as in *Farewell* but also in the narrative itself. It is full of soldier-language expressions: "… ein Kochgeschirr voll [Essen] fassen; sich hinhauen; dicke Brocken; Gulaschmarie."—In other instances the language becomes, particularly in the beginning, colloquial; for instance: "Er bietet das Essen *direkt* an; er weiss nicht, wie er seine Gulaschkanone *leerkriegen* soll; sie würden einen *schönen* Schrekken *kriegen*."—Such expressions are proper in the actual conversation but bothersome in the narrative because they disrupt its unity. In other parts it is difficult to decide whether the language is inadequate or whether it is the substance as such that is insufficient. There are numerous passages, particularly in the beginning of the novel, where the narrator thinks about the situation he has just told. For instance, in the first chapter, after coming back from the front, the group of friends play cards together:

> Man könnte ewig so sitzen.
>   Die Töne einer Ziehharmonika klingen von den Baracken her. Manchmal legen wir die Karten hin und sehen uns an. Einer sagt dann: "Kinder, Kinder——," oder: "Das hätte schiefgehen können—," und wir versinken einen Augenblick in Schweigen.

Up to here the description of the atmosphere is good and, in fact, contains everything pointed out in the following lines which are not only superfluous but even embarrassing:

> In uns ist ein starkes, verhaltenes Gefühl, jeder spürt es, das braucht nicht viele Worte. Leicht hätte, es sein können, dass wir heute nicht auf unseren Kästen sässen es war verdammt nahe daran.

The same thing is wrong with the paragraph in which Remarque deals with the attitude of the young soldiers toward the older generation:

> Sie sollten uns Achtzehnjährigen Vermittler und Führer zur Welt des Erwachsenenseins werden, zur Welt der Arbeit, der Pflicht, der Kultur und des Fortschritts, zur Zukunft.

Here Remarque's opinion is not dramatized, is not action or situation and therefore unsatisfactory. It appears that paragraphs like this could be left out without any loss of substance because the same subject matter is contained in the grotesque scene where the soldiers imitate their former teachers. Here everything is vivid situation showing with intensity the enormous gap between the school situation and war life.

It seems that the language of the novel becomes better—or has fewer inadequacies—as the story unfolds. Whether Remarque describes instances of every-day life, the experiences of Paul when alone on guard or when at home, an attack prepared by hours and hours of endless bombardment, whether he gives a dialogue of the soldiers about the causes of war, the picture created is of a vividness and directness which the reader cannot escape. One example is the description of the artillery and gas attack. In short sentences, which are not complete in critical moments, the scene is given with precision and with great power and imagination for pictures to describe the indescribable:

> Wir kommen in die Laufgräben und dann in die Wiesen. Das Wäldchen taucht auf; wir kennen hier jeden Schritt Boden . . .
> In der nächsten Minute hebt sich ein Stück Wald unter einem zweiten Einschlag langsam über die Gipfel, drei, vier Bäume segeln mit und brechen dabei in Stücke . . . Das Dunkel wird wahnsinning. Es wogt und tobt. Schwärzere Dunkelheiten als die Nacht rasen mit Riesenbuckeln auf uns los, über uns hinweg . . . Ich spüre einen Ruck . . . Ich balle die Faust. Keine Schmerzen.

Or after two days and two nights of continuous bombardment he says of the group in the dugout:

> Noch eine Nacht. Wir sind jetzt stumpf vor Spannung. Es ist eine tödliche Spannung, die wie ein schartiges Messer unser Rückenmark entlang kratzt. Die Beine wollen nicht mehr, die Hände zittern, der Körper ist eine dünne Haut über mühsam unterdrücktem Wahnsinn, über einem gleich hemmungslos ausbrechenden Gebrüll ohne Ende.

In chapter eleven, a simple enumeration of words is found, not even sentences, that remind of Hemingway's programmatic passage: "Certain numbers were the same way and certain dates and these with the names of the places were all you could say and have them mean anything." After Remarque has established rapport with the reader, he enumerates diseases and other possibilities for the soldier to die:

> Granaten, Gasschwaden und Tankflotillen—Zerstampfen, Zerfressen, Tod.
> Ruhr, Grippe, Typhus—Würgen, Verbrennen, Tod.
> Graben, Lazarett, Massengrab—mehr Möglichkeiten gibt es nicht.

In passages like this one it appears that Remarque achieves a greater intensity than Hemingway in the field of the war novel.

But not only in passages of high tension does Remarque reach high intensity and adequate language. For instance when Paul comes home after the experiences of the front, he sees the scenery near his home town. The contrast of this picture of peace in those simple words and sentences is overwhelming. The same is true for some of the lyric passages about Paul's stay in the training camp.

As to the structure of the two novels, it might be expected that Hemingway's has a clearer and more artistic arrangement. There are five distinct parts, given in the five books. The central book, the third, contains the title event, Frederic Henry's farewell to arms. Philip Young has pointed out how the novel is built with scrupulous care, how Henry's affair with the war goes through six phases as Catherine's affair with him goes through the same number in a parallel fashion.

The action of Remarque's story does not run along such strict lines of symmetry, although it might be well to point out certain similarities. The novel has twelve chapters of which the sixth and the seventh are especially long. The first and the last five chapters have approximately the same number of pages. But also from the point of view of content chapters six and seven are the center of the book. Chapters one through five prepare the reader for the central chapters through the description of various aspects of life in and closely behind the front line as well as through portraying the soldiers in their attitude to and isolation from their former civilian world. Chapter six, then, starts with Bäumer's company being moved, past a huge wall of coffins, to the front line, tells of the fight against the rats, of details about weapons for hand-to-hand fighting, describes the tension of the calm days during which supplies are heard to be brought in on the other side, and then the days and nights of heavy bombardment, the cracking of the inexperienced soldiers, attack, counterattack, the bloody details of combat, the cries and slow deaths of wounded soldiers between the lines, the smell of rotting flesh, the return to the rest camp two weeks later:

> Der Morgen ist grau, es war noch Sommer, als wir hinausgingen, und wir waren 150 Mann. Jetzt friert uns, es ist Herbst, die Blätter rascheln, . . .
> Eine Reihe, eine kurze Reihe tappt in den Morgen hinaus. Zweiund-dreissig Mann.

It is precisely the kind of war depicted in this chapter that made World War One the first modern war and different from all previous wars, a war in which a whole generation was sacrificed in such battles as that of Verdun and the Somme. In Remarque's novel it reads thus:

> Doch das Stückehen zerwühlter Erde, in dem wir liegen, ist

gehalten gegen die Übermacht, nur wenige hundert Meter sind preisgegeben worden. Aber auf jeden Meter kommt ein Toter.

The terror of chapter six is complemented by Bäumer's experiences on leave at home which most of chapter seven is devoted to. The soldier returns to that world which used to be his home and with which he has been trying to reconcile the new realities of the world of war ever since he was sent into it. He finds an invisible wall between himself and his parents, his teachers, and everybody and everything at home. There is no way back. The peak in this sequence of scenes is that in which he meets his former teachers who treat him to some beer and some good advice. The principal is determined to annex Belgium, parts of France and Russia and knows how the enemy can be overcome. He proves to Bäumer that he really does not know anything about the war, that his point of view is too limited:

> Gewiss, der einzelne, . . . aber es kommt doch auf das Gesamte an. Und das können Sie nicht so beurteilen. Sie sehen nur Ihren kleinen Abschnitt und haben deshalb keine Übersicht. Sie tun Ihre Pflicht, Sie setzen Ihr Leben ein, das ist höchster Ehren wert—jeder von Euch müsste das Eiserne Kreuz haben —, aber vor allem muss die gegnerische Front in Flandern durchbrochen und dann von oben aufgerollt werden.

Against the content of the previous chapter, this conversation is grotesque and proves that Bäumer is really alone in such surroundings. He even has a certain longing to go back to his platoon.

The novel is built around these two chapters that contain its central conflict: that between the new realities of the war and the values and traditions of Paul Bäumer's past as a civilian. It is the tension between these two worlds that provides another structural element of the novel that is also closely connected with the development of character. In the beginning Bäumer mentions again and again his old class, the school, the teachers, and the adult world to which these supposedly were their guides. In the course of the story these passages about school and home become shorter and less frequent, the new reality of the war asserts itself more and more. Graphically it would be something like this:

war ———   ———   ———   ———   ———
past   ——   ——   —   —

In chapter ten, for instance, Bäumer is frightened by the soldiers' lack of emotion, by their being utterly objective:

So sachlich, dass mir manchmal graut, wenn einen Augenblicke in Gedanke aus der früheren Zeit, vor dem Kriege, sich in meinen Kopf verirrt. Er bleibt auch nicht lange.

Or in chapter eleven he describes the extreme simplicity of constantly living on the verge of death:

Das ist die einzige Art, uns zu retten, und oft sitze ich vor mir selber wie vor einem Fremden, wenn der rätselhafte Widerschein des Früher in stillen Stunden wie ein matter Spiegel die Umrisse meines jetzigen Daseins ausser mich stellt, . . .

Now, towards the end of the novel, the former life and world only come as a stray thought that does not stay, the reflection of the past is enigmatic, the two worlds in himself have become strangers. The last link in this chain is one bitter sentence after the death of Leer: "Was nützt es ihm nun, dass er in der Schule ein so guter Mathematicker war."—The answer is clear, although it is not stated: NOTHING! It seems to imply a similar answer to the question that has been asked all through the novel: what is our culture good for if it permits this war to go on?

The change in the pattern just discussed reflects a character development of Paul which is partly given in retrospect. The reader becomes aware of a change which takes and has already taken place in the character of Paul: from the high school student full of plans and idealistic aims over the soldier who tries to solve the problem of incongruity between his background and the reality of war, whose thoughts return again and again to this problem, to the soldier whose entire energy is concentrated on survival and who finally gives in to the certainty of being alone and lost. What is reached here at the end of a long succession of terrible experiences seems to be present in the character of Lt. Henry from the beginning. His experiences are not related to any past as a civilian. In chapter three for instance there is already the attitude which is typical for Hemingway's "lost generation":

I had gone to no such place [the Abruzzi] but to the smoke of cafés and nights when the room whirled and you needed to look at the wall to make it stop, nights in bed, drunk, when you knew that that was all there was, and the strange excitement of waking and not knowing who it was with you . . . and not caring in the night . . . Suddenly to care very much.

Frederic has this attitude when he meets Catherine. Slowly real love grows in him. He tries to flee from the unwholesome world of the war into the love of

Catherine. With his escape to Switzerland the war story proper ends although the same set of symbols continues. This continuation seems to suggest that Hemingway, in this novel, sees not only war but the entire human existence under the aspect of chance. It is to be noted, though, that some critics have found this part of the book least convincing. But since we are mainly interested in *Farewell* as a war story, this part need not be of major concern to us.

Halliday discusses the use of irony in *Farewell* and maintains that it has a "predominantly ironic texture." Some of his observations seem to be well made: the use of "only" in "only seven thousand died of the cholera" is ironical; so is that everything functions well without Lt. Henry while he is on leave, that he gets a silver medal although he was eating spaghetti and cheese when he was wounded, and so is the portrait of Ettore, the legitimate hero. But it is difficult to see how the disproportion of Henry's comparatively good life in the army and his being malcontent is ironical, as it is difficult to find an ironic parallel in the military justice Henry deals the sergeant and the one he is dealt at the bridge. I find the occasional use of irony in *Farewell* rather similar to that of *Im Westen*. When the company come back from the front where they have lost about half their men, they receive, because of poor communication, double rations. Tjaden's comment is: "Das nennt man Schwein haben." Or there is the scene with the former teachers who have all sort of good advice for the soldier. The irony of the situation is obvious as the words take on a different meaning for the reader than they have for the speaker. Finally there is the irony in the title of either novel. Henry's farewell to the army suddenly turns into a farewell to Catherine's arms. The violence and chaos of the war is shown as one of the conditions of life in general. Ironically the title takes on a new meaning. The irony Remarque uses in the title of his novel is slightly different. The title phrase appears in the final scene of the book:

> Er fiel im Oktober 1918, an einem Tage, der so ruhig und
> still war an der ganzen Front, dass der Heeresbericht sich nur auf
> den Satz beschränkte, im Westen sei nichts Neues zu melden.

The reader is hit with the news of Bäumer's death under the motto of "nothing new." The killing of a man "nothing new"? Hardly, since for four years many had been killed like Paul Bäumer. However, "nothing new" is not only the title for the last scene but for the entire book. And thus it takes on another meaning, namely the exact opposite—this book describes something very new, a new kind of war, the butchering of an entire generation, the bankruptcy of a civilization. The title is cutting, bitter irony.

After these technical and rather formal points of view a comparison of contents seems to be in order. There are many parallel points in the novels:

both contain hospital scenes, the chief character is wounded, the conversation concentrates either around food or women, the soldiers talk about the causes of war, partly even with the same arguments. It appears to be profitable to explore some of these aspects in greater detail.

Frederick J. Hoffman interprets much of *Farewell* in terms of Lt. Henry's wound, not only a physical but also a psychic wound that profoundly upsets his relationship with his own past and that of society to which he belongs, a problem that also was at the center of Remarque's novel. The same psychic wound appears here:

> Wir waren achtzehn Jahre und begannen die Welt und das Dasein zu lieben; wir mussten darauf schiessen. Die erste Granate, die einschlug traf in unser Herz. Wir sind abgeschlossen vom Tätigen, vom Streben, vom Fortschritt. Wir glauben nicht mehr daran; wir glauben an den Krieg.

According to Hoffman, it is this wound that gives Henry a deep distrust of those who try to explain, to give assurances. "They don't know what they are talking about." Remarque's novel, at one point, almost reads like a commentary to *Farewell*:

> Während sie noch schrieben und redeten, sahen wir Lazarette und Sterbende,—während sie den Dienst am Staate als das Grösste bezeichneten, wussten wir bereits, dass die Todesangst stärker ist. Wir wurden darum keine Meuterer . . . aber wir unterschieden jetzt, wir hatten mit einem Male sehen gelernt.

One will easily catch the contrast between "wir" and "sie" in the above quote. "We" had learned to "see." This is quite similar to the "realizing" the priest talks about: "Many people have realized the war this summer. Officers whom I thought could never realize it realize it now." In Hemingway criticism it is called "awareness." Those who "see," who "realize" things belong. When Frederic comes back and meets Rinaldi, when Paul comes back and meets the friends of his group, it is not the many words that count, but the feeling that there is a wordless understanding: "I was glad to see Rinaldi again. He had spent two years teasing me and I had always liked it. We understood each other very well." The impossibility of communicating with the outsiders becomes obvious when Henry ponders about writing home: "There was nothing to write about. I sent a couple of army Zona di Guerra postcards, crossing out everything except, I am well. That should handle them." When Paul is at home, he says: "Hier und da spricht mich jemand an. Ich halte mich nicht lange auf, denn ich will nicht soviel reden." Or in the training camp afterwards: "Und ich habe hier nicht viel Anschluss, wünsche ihn auch nicht über das normale Mass hinaus. Man ist zu wenig miteinander bekannt." There is no bridge of understanding to those who do not belong.

Not all soldiers automatically belong. When Ettore brags that he "shot that son of a bitch all right" or when sergeant Oellrich as a sniper marks down each hit with such exclamations as "Das hat gessen!" "Hast du gesehen, wie er hochsprang?," the reader realizes that they have never learned to "see."

Another set of parallel ideas one finds under the catchword of "thinking" or rather "not thinking." Philip Young, when talking about Lt. Henry, sums it up in: ". . . and this is again the old protagonist, who cannot sleep at night for thinking—who must not use his head to think with, and will absolutely have to stop it." A similar attitude toward thinking can be found in Remarque's novel. In the first chapter the life in the rest camp is described: "Es sind wunderbar gedankenlose Stunden." More explicitly he talks about it after the great battle in chapter six:

> Solange wir hier im Felde sein müssen, sinken die Fronttage, wenn sie vorbei sind, wie Steine in uns hinunter, weil sie zu schwer sind, um sofort darüber nachdenken zu können. Täten wir es, sie würden uns hinterher erschlagen; denn soviel habe ich schon gemerkt: Das Grauen lässt sich ertragen, solange man sich einfach duckt—aber es tötet, wenn man darüber nachdenkt.

The same idea is expressed when Bäumer, at home, refuses to talk about the war and reasons with himself about it:

> . . . es ist eine Gefahr für mich, wenn ich diese Dinge in Worte bringe, ich habe Scheu, dass sie dann riesenhaft werden und sich nicht mehr bewältigen lassen. Wo blieben wir, wenn uns alles ganz klar würde, was da draussen vorgeht.

Lt. Henry and Paul Bäumer are actively refusing to think. Remarque is more explicit concerning the reasons: the effort not to think is necessary for survival. It is a defense mechanism of man constantly living on the verge of death and deeply involved in killing. But it is not the only one. Henry tries to stay out of a searing dream. Bäumer realizes how thin the wall is that protects him from darkness and disintegration when he awakes out of a dream:

> . . . empfindet man nachts,—aus einem Traum aufwachend, überwältigt und preisgegeben . . . , wie dünn der Halt und die Grenze ist, die uns von der Dunkelheit trennt— . . . notdürftig

geschützt durch schwache Wände vor dem Sturm der Auflösung
und der Sinnlosigkeit . . .

The thin protection against disintegration and chaos has to be preserved by
all means. Only the simplest form of life can be sustained under these
circumstances. Remarque calls it a "geschlossenes, hartes Dasein äusserster
Oberfläche." Or he finds that the life of these soldiers is on the level of
animals: "Aus uns sind gefährliche Tiere geworden. . . . Genau wie wir zu
Tieren werden, wenn wir nach vorn gehen . . . es hat uns zu denkenden
Tieren gemacht . . ." It is the utmost primitivity that saves the soldier from
losing his mind, his life, or both:

> Das Leben hier an der Grenze des Todes hat eine ungeheuer
> einfache Linie, es beschränkt sich auf das Notwendigste . . . das ist
> unsere Primitivität und unsere Rettung. Wären wir differenzierter,
> wir wären, längst irrsinnig, desertiert oder gefallen.

The soldier's grim jokes, his understatement in talking about death or
sentiment in general, have the same purpose:

> Das Grauen der Front versinkt, wenn wir ihm den Rücken
> kehren, wir gehen ihm mit gemeinen und grimmigen Witzen zu
> Leibe; wenn jemand stirbt, dann heisst es, dass er den Arsch
> zugekniffen hat, und so reden wir über alles, das rettet uns vor
> dem Verrücktweden . . .

And it is in the same light that the comradeship, the attachment to one
another of those who belong is to be understood. Warren points out that
Henry's obligation is not one to the total war but to the men in his immediate
command and that they are bound together only by a squad sense and their
respect for one another. Bäumer feels a similar obligation to the men of his
group. Elshorst says about Remarque:

> Im Kampf um die nackte Existenz bewähren sich, wie im
> Krieg, ursprüngliche menschliche Tugenden, an die Remarque
> unbeirrbar glaubt: Kameradschaft, Hillfsbereitschaft. Liebe.

However, it should not be forgotten how these virtues appear in the novel
proper; toward the end, the author sums up:

> Est ist eine grosse Brüderschaft, die einen Schimmer von
> dem Kameradentum der Volkslieder, dem Solidaritätsgefühl von

> Sträflingen und dem verzweifelten Einanderbeistehen von zum
> Tode Verurteilten seltsam vereinigt . . .

and adds a little later:

> . . . es [das Leben] hat uns zu denkenden Tieren gemacht, um uns
> die Waffe des Instinktes zu geben—es hat uns mit Stumpfheit
> durchsetzt, damit wir nicht zerbrechen vor dem Grauen . . . —es
> hat in uns den Kameradschaftssinn geweckt, damit wir dem
> Abgrund der Verlassenheit entgehen . . . Wir unterscheiden uns
> äusserlich in der Lebensform kaum von Buschnegern; aber
> während diese stets so sein können . . . ist es bei uns umgekehrt;
> unsere inneren Kräfte sind nicht auf Weiter—, sondern auf
> Zurückentwicklung angespannt.

The last quote particularly shows the way in which Remarque wants these "virtues"—comradeship, primitive (primal) emotions, understatement, lack of sentiment, lack of sophistication, etc.—understood: they are only the means toward a possible survival and indicate at the same time the bankruptcy of a civilization, a regrettable retrogression (Zurückentwicklung). It seems that this aspect should be borne in mind and might also be fruitful for appreciating the less explicit Hemingway novel. It may well be that some critics have seen too much celebration of the physical and simple in Hemingway rather than the artistically exquisite, but nevertheless sad account of a cultural retrogression.

Finally some other parallels should be noted in passing. Hemingway makes autumn a leitmotif of the story. Remarque uses it at the end of the central sixth chapter. In both novels the men of the group have a discussion about the origin and meaning of this war. The attitudes of both authors are so obviously alike that a few short examples are sufficient. The statement of Hemingway starting "I was always embarrassed by the words sacred, glorious, and sacrifice . . ." is true for both novels alike. Both stress that side of the war which was, at that time, not the official one: the unheroic, dirty, painful, bloody side of it. The word "heroism" is hardly ever heard and if at all, then mostly in the absurd sense of cheap patriotism.

In most cases Remarque's discussion of any of these aspects of war is much more detailed and in most cases his characters are much more involved than those of Hemingway. For instance there is the hospital scene with Kemmerich who was one of the group: Remarque describes how his face slowly changes into the mask of death. The impressiveness is intensified by telling of Franz's departure from home and of Müller's negotiations about his wonderful English shoes even before Franz is dead. When Hemingway speaks about the dressing station, he gives a rather general picture: "The doctors were working with their sleeves up to their shoulders and were red as butchers." When Lt. Henry is worked upon, he tells the medical details thus holding back the personal remarks. The hospital in Milan is a Swiss hotel compared to the German "Lazarett." The moments of actual danger in *Farewell* are comparatively few and short. In Remarque's story on the other hand there is the gas attack, the continuous bombardment for several days and nights, then the attack, and finally the company is transported to the rest camp; when they are counted, they find out that of 150 men who went out 32 are left. In its shortness and simplicity this last scene is extremely effective. Or there are Paul's experiences between the lines with the attack of the enemy rolling over him, the Frenchman jumping into the same funnel and Paul stabbing him, staying for hours together with the dying man. Many of such scenes, if given at all, are only germinal in Hemingway's story.

In many instances the Remarque novel is much more comprehensive as a war novel because it includes so many more aspects of war than Hemingway's. Just to give a few examples: the every-day drudgery of military life is referred to in the sergeant-Himmelstoss scenes or in the lice-killing action. Or there are the encounters with the Russian prisoners of war. Indicative for the worse German position is that food is of such great importance—life is reduced to the most primitive of all instincts. The soldiers in the Hemingway story stand one step higher: they are most interested in whoring and drinking. Or there is Paul on leave at home where the absurdity of flag-waving patriotism is fully developed and the abyss between those patriots and the front soldier is shown. There is the suffering of the wounded and dying horses, the suffering of a wounded man who lies between the lines for two days, always calling for help and slowly dying—alone. More examples could be found easily.

It is not surprising that, to a certain degree, the fate of the two novels after publication showed some parallels too. When, from May to October 1929, *Farewell* appeared in *Scribner's Magazine*, the June and July issues of the magazine were banned in Boston by the Chief of Police. Warren reports that there were objections to the book from various quarters. It was called "dirty, immoral, disgusting, garbage." The book and the film both were banned in Italy by the Mussolini government because they supposedly did not do justice to the Italian soldier. For much the same reason *Im Westen* was prohibited and burned in Germany after the Nazi takeover. In the public ceremony, these were the words of the announcer as the novel was thrown into the flames: "Gegen literarischen Verrat am Soldaten des Weltkrieges, für Erziehung des Volkes im Geiste der Wahrhaftigkeit! Ich übergebe der

Flamme die Schriften von Erich Maria Remarque." When the film was shown in December 1930 in Berlin, the Nazis started riots so that the showings had to be discontinued. On December 11, 1930 the film was forbidden for all of Germany.

The preceding discussion shows a large number of parallels between Remarque's *Im Westen nichts Neues* and Hemingway's *A Farewell to Arms*, parallels of technique as well as of content. It might be safely said that, from the point of view of technique, *Farewell* is superior although *Im Westen* shows substantial accomplishments in the same directions and is by no means an artless novel. This was demonstrated, for instance, in the use of irony, symbolism, and in the structure of the novels.

From the point of view of content *Im Westen* appears as a substantially more comprehensive war novel. Many aspects of war are present only in a germinal fashion in Hemingway's book whereas they receive a much more thorough treatment in that of Remarque. Lt. Henry's experience is, in a way, that of his country as a whole. It reflects the development from wholehearted participation to escape, from Wilson to Harding. Such an escape is unthinkable for Paul Bäumer. Accordingly, the commitment of Germany during that war was incomparably more serious. But in spite of these differences, the attitudes of both authors to World War One, their experiencing the war show a great deal of similarity. It appears significant that the tenor of these two classics about World War One, although written by authors whose countries were at war with each other, should be so similar that the short preface of *Im Westen nichts Neues* might well be applied to *A Farewell to Arms*: "Dieses Buch soll weder eine Anklage noch ein Bekenntnis sein. Es soll nur den Versuch machen, über eine Generation zu berichtnen, die vom Kriege zerstört wurde—auch wenn sie seinen Granaten entkam."

WILHELM J. SCHWARZ

The Works of Ernst Jünger and Erich Maria Remarque on World War I

Ernst Jünger's *In Stahlgewittern*, his war diary about the first World War, is the *Hohelied*, the apotheosis, of heroic, authoritarian leadership. It is the story of the author who, at the age of nineteen, leaves school in the torrent of enthusiasm that sweeps over Germany at the outbreak of the war in August, 1914, to enlist as a volunteer. Having grown up in an age of security, peace and stability, he feels a yearning for the unusual, for adventure, and for intense, dangerous experience. After a few weeks of training he leaves for the front in a deluge of flowers, "in einer trunkenen Stimmung von Rosen und Blut" (in an intoxicated mood of roses and blood). The war is hailed as the occasion for manly deeds, for greatness, strength and solemn grandeur. The ecstatic mood of the young recruit, however, soon gives way to a somewhat more reflective attitude toward the war, especially after he sees the first victims of battle. Nevertheless, the war retains for him, on the whole, its august, sublime, almost sacred, *éclat* until the very end.

The author spends four long years, with few interruptions, in the front lines. He is genuinely despondent when forced to miss an engagement or a battle. On one occasion, while taking a short course away from his company, he hears about the great losses sustained by his unit and is deeply disturbed because he had to be away from his comrades at such a time. Brave and daring officers win his unreserved admiration. Fourteen times he is seriously wounded,

From *War and the Mind of Germany*. © 1975 Herbert Lang & Co. Ltd. and Peter Lang Ltd.

receiving a total of twenty scars. A fearless, audacious fighter, he earns the highest war medal that the Second Empire awards, the *Ordre pour le mérite*.

Ernst Jünger, in his person, presents to the reader the phenomenon of an Odysseus who becomes his own Homer. In chiseled language the author pictures himself as an adventurous, valiant officer and as the representative of the German officers of World War I who fought courageously at the front for four years.

As Jünger's war diary could be considered a monument to the heroic leader, so *Im Westen nichts Neues* by Erich Maria Remarque might be called a memorial to the unknown soldier. Paul Bäumer, the hero of Remarque's book, also joins the armed forces as an eighteen-year-old volunteer. His teacher, Kantorek, delivers fervent patriotic speeches until the whole class of twenty students with idealistic and romantic views about life and war march to the *Bezirkskommando* to sign up. Only one student, Josef Behm, a good-natured boy, wavers. The others finally persuade him to enlist also. Perhaps there are other boys who think as he does. But nobody can stand back at a time when even parents are inclined to use the word "coward."

Strange to say, Josef Behm is the first one to die in action. During an attack on the enemy lines he is shot in the eyes and abandoned for dead. In the afternoon he begins to call for help and crawls frantically around between the lines without sense of direction. Wild with excruciating pain and unable to see, he fails to take cover and is shot by the French before anybody can go to bring him in. Remarque raises the question of responsibility for the death of this boy, one of many who had to die before they had begun to live.

Im Westen nichts Neues opens with the statement that the book is neither an accusation nor a creed but only an attempt to report on a generation of men who were destroyed by the war even though they may have escaped its grenades. Yet this book is an accusation of the older generation who let loose this terrible catastrophe, this monstrous war. It is an accusation of the generation that preached that service to the state was the highest aim in life.

On the battlefield in Belgium and France, German youth is emancipated from the *Weltanschauung* of the older generation. Remarque states:

> Während sie noch schrieben und redeten, sahen wir Lazarette und Sterbende; —während sie den Dienst am Staate als das Grösste bezeichneten, wussten wir bereits, dass die Todesangst stärker ist. Wir wurden darum keine Meuterer, keine Deserteure, keine Feiglinge—alle diese Ausdrücke waren ihnen ja so leicht zur Hand—, wir liebten unsere Heimat genau so wie sie, und wir gingen bei jedem Angriff mutig vor; —aber wir unterschieden jetzt, wir hatten mit einem Male sehen gelernt. Und wir sahen,

dass nichts von ihrer Welt übrig blieb. Wir waren plötzlich auf eine furchtbare Weise allein und wir mussten allein damit fertig werden.

(While they were still writing and talking, we saw the wounded and the dying. While they called service to the state the greatest thing, we knew already that the fear of death is stronger. We did not become mutineers, deserters or cowards because of this—all these expressions were freely used by them—we loved our homeland as much as they and we went courageously into each attack. But now we differentiated. All of a sudden we had learned to see. And we saw that nothing of their world was left. We were suddenly terribly alone and alone we had to cope with it.)

Jünger, of course, encounters no problem of this nature. At least there is no indication of it in his writings. He gladly accepts the whole system of German militarism from his sergeant to his Kaiser. He is a soldier and executes the orders of his superiors without questioning their authority. Of high personal integrity, he does his duty conscientiously and punctiliously. He makes his whole existence unconditionally subservient to the need of his country. While being sent to Heidelberg for treatment of an injury he reflects: "Wie schön war doch das Land, wohl wert, dafür zu bluten und zu sterben." (How beautiful the country was, well worth bleeding and dying for.) While recuperating from another wound in a military hospital, he gives the whole of his possessions, three thousand marks, to the state in the form of a *Kriegsanleihe*, a war bond.

Apart from the above cited passage and the love of country it reflects there is scarcely any indication that Jünger is concerned with the causes of the war, its aims and justification, its legitimacy or its absurdity. Basically he sees in the war only an unparalleled chance for adventure, an opportunity to unleash all his hidden Viking instincts. After he has become a lieutenant—to the privates in the Kaiser's army a rank comparable to that of a demi-god—he leads his men and treats his enemies as would a knight of old. Once, while skulking around on hands and knees in no man's land between the German and Anglo-French lines, he remembers episodes in Karl May's adventure books. He gallantly and chivalrously acknowledges the great fighting qualities of the enemy, particularly of the English and Scottish troops, and mentions with sincere respect several incidents of personal bravery on the British side.

But even the front line, with all its attacks and counterattacks, does not give sufficient scope for his unquenchable thirst for action. Consequently he picks a few like-minded knights of fortune and pays the enemy, in his own trenches, a few private visits, leaving slaughter and butchery in his wake. "Wir hatten kein anderes Ziel im Auge als etwas zwischen den Drähten herumzustreichen und zu sehen, was uns das Niemandsland Neues brächte, denn die Stellung begann allmählich wieder langweilig zu werden." (We had no other aim than to linger around between the barbed wires and to see what novelties no man's land might offer, since the trenches began to be boring again.)

Such ambitions, of course, are foreign to Paul Bäumer, or Remarque. Bäumer's enthusiasm for the army, for the war, for heroism and all types of military activity is crushed and squelched in the barracks, never to be revived again. One morning he has to make his bed fourteen times for Corporal Himmelstoss. He has to scrub the corporal's mess with a toothbrush. He has to remove the snow from the yard of the barracks with a handbrush and a dustpan. Sarcastically he states that he is becoming an unequalled master of *Kniebeugen*, of knee-bending. The life in the barracks, where a former mailman, now in the uniform of a corporal, is wielding almost unlimited power over a group of fear-ridden boys, breaks his idealism and all his illusions about the "great time." "Wir lernten, dass ein geputzter Knopf wichtiger ist als vier Bände Schopenhauer. . . . Mit Begeisterung und gutem Willen waren wir Soldaten geworden; aber man tat alles, um uns das auszutreiben." (We learned that a polished button is more important than four volumes of Schopenhauer. . . . We became soldiers with enthusiasm and good-will but they did everything to knock that out of us.) And yet, there comes a time when he almost yearningly looks back to this period of human degradation. This is the time of the great slaughters and massacres.

Death for the fatherland, death "auf blumigen, blutbetauten Wiesen" (on flowery, blood-bedewed meadows), as Jünger calls it, has no charm for Remarque. Paul Bäumer sees his friends die, one after the other. He sees those who are poisoned by gas vomit up bits of their burnt lungs during long weeks of indescribable agony. Wounded soldiers, deserted by friend and foe, lie in no man's land and sometimes die only after endless hours of lonely suffering. Remarque has no enthusiasm for the glorious "Tod fürs Vaterland," death for the fatherland. Again and again comes the accusation of the older generation, in spite of the statement on the first page that the book is not meant to be an accusation. Bäumer watches his school-friend, Franz Kemmerich, die after the amputation of his leg has not brought the expected results.

Franz Kemmerich sah beim Baden klein und schmal aus wie ein Kind. Da liegt er nun, weshalb nur? Man sollte die ganze Welt an diesem Bette vorbeiführen und sagen: Das ist Franz Kemmerich, neunzehneinhalb Jahre alt, er will nicht sterben. Lasst ihn nicht sterben!

(While bathing, Franz Kemmerich used to look little and frail like a child. There he lies now, but why? One should lead the whole world past this bed and say, 'That is Franz Kemmerich, nineteen and a half years old. He does not want to die. Don't let him die!')

Death has no horrors for Jünger. During a lull a sentinel suddenly falls to the ground with a shot in the head. The corpse is carried away by the ambulance men. As soon as they disappear, someone shovels some dirt on the bloody spot and everything is the same as before. Jünger does not shoot at the enemy simply because this is the order; he also finds a certain satisfaction in it. He and his friends devise all sorts of tricks to kill a few enemies during the quiet periods on the front. "Manche sind mit weidmännischem Eifer bei der Sache. . . . Ihnen macht der Krieg eben Spass." (Some are at the job with a sportsmanlike eagerness. . . . They simply enjoy the war.) Without comment he mentions that in the little French town of Combles he sees a small girl lying in a pool of blood in front of the threshold of a house. In Monchy he notices a line of gassed soldiers, groaning, vomiting and choking, some of whom die after suffering excruciating pain. The same evening he sits with his friends around a fire, singing, smoking and drinking. War is War. In September, 1915, he becomes an officer cadet and soon afterwards second lieutenant. During the rest of the war he serves as shock-troop officer, employed in all daring and dangerous enterprises in this particular front area. The adventurer, who only one year before the war ran away from home to join the French Foreign Legion, has finally found a suitable sphere of action.

* * * * * *

Completely absorbed in the business of fighting, Jünger makes little mention of his family or earlier life. Only once in the whole book does he refer to his mother. In July, 1917, the English break through the German lines at Langemarck after a murderous, devastating bombardment. Jünger receives the message that his brother Friedrich lies critically wounded in a nearby dugout, already deserted by the Germans. Amidst a number of groaning, dying men in a room permeated by a cadaverous stench he finds Friedrich, his lung pierced by one shrapnel bullet and his shoulder joint smashed by another. He is delirious but still conscious. Jünger orders five of his men to take his brother through the inferno of bursting shells into safety. "Ich fühlte mich zugleich als Vertreter meiner Mutter und ihr für das Schicksal meines Bruders verantwortlich." (I felt myself as the representative of my mother and at the same time responsible to her for the fate of my brother.) Friedrich Jünger is brought to a military hospital and eventually cured, although his shoulder remains stiff for the rest of his life. This incident is the only indication in the whole book that Jünger has any affection for members of his family.

Women do not play any role at all in Jünger's war diaries. It is true that a French girl invites him for supper on one occasion. If any intimate relations develop he does not mention them, although he describes the meal with meticulous care: eggs, white bread and butter, lying very appetizingly on a cabbage leaf. In the town of Brancourt he is lodged with a French couple and their very pretty daughter. One day, quite accidentally, he encounters her when she is nude—to the embarrassment of both. But he shows no further interest in her. There is no indication that he has any relations, however harmless, with a girl in Germany. He is a warrior made of Krupp steel. In his spare time he reads, with great pleasure, the whole of Ariosto's writings.

Paul Bäumer is not a warrior. He is simply a human creature. He has exchanged the world of his youth for this nightmare of hell upon earth:

> Trommelfeuer, Sperrfeuer, Gardinenfeuer, Minen, Gas, Tanks, Maschinengewehre, Handgranaten—Worte, Worte, aber sie umfassen das Grauen der Welt. Unsere Gesichter sind verkrustet, unser Denken ist verwüstet, wir sind todmüde—wenn der Angriff kommt, müssen manche mit den Fäusten geschlagen werden, damit sie erwachen und mitgehen.

> (Drum-fire, barrage-fire, curtain-fire, mines, gas, tanks, machine-guns, hand-grenades—words, words, but they encompass the horror of the world. Our faces are scabby, our thinking is laid waste, we are dead-tired—when the attack comes, some need to be beaten with fists so that they will wake up and come along.)

Year after year he listens to the whining of the shells and only sometimes—when he feels the air warmly and softly caressing his face—does he think about girls and blooming meadows and white clouds and about his irrevocably lost youth.

Paul stands with his friend, Albert, in front of a big poster giving notice about a troupe that is to visit the fighting units. Depicted on the poster is a girl in a bright summer dress and white shoes. "Es ist ein ganz herrliches Mädchen, mit einer schmalen Nase, mit roten Lippen und langen Beinen, unvorstellbar sauber und gepflegt, es badet gewiss zweimal am Tage und hat nie Dreck unter den Nägeln." (She is an extremely beautiful girl, with a thin nose, red lips and long legs, unbelievably clean and well-groomed. She certainly bathes twice a day and never has dirt under her finger nails.) They find it hard to understand that this is a picture of a girl who really exists, a girl of flesh and blood.

And then he meets a French girl, a gentle, small, dark young woman who strokes his hair and says, "La guerre—grand malheur—pauvres garçons." And he feels her lips and he closes his eyes and he tries to wipe it all out, the war and the horror and the vulgarity, tries to become young and happy again. And he hopes for a miracle, an escape from the world of mud, and blood, and gas, and brothels before which the soldiers stand in a long queue.

* * * * * *

Jünger displays no sentiment or nostalgia with regard to his youth. He does not miss the friendship or love of women. His dreams find their fulfillment in the trenches. Here he feels himself a prince in his domain. He takes his meals alone or in company with other officers, aristocrats of the war, waited on by a faithful and devoted orderly. During some attacks and hand-to-hand fighting in the enemy lines, he wears only a silken cap instead of the steel helmet, carries a horsewhip or a walking stick and, according to regulations, wears a long coat and officers' gloves in spite of the great heat. During a perilous and spectacular attack on the enemy lines, instigated by a drunken officer, he and eighty of his men capture about two hundred prisoners and a considerable amount of war material. The same evening he reports to his colonel.

> Nachdem ich halb im Schlaf, aber in vorzüglicher Stimmung mit ihm [dem Oberst] eine Flasche Wein geleert hatte, verabaschiedete ich mich und warf mich nach diesem gewaltigen Tage mit einem Feierabendgefühl in das Bett, das mir mein treuer Vinke bereitet hatte.

> (After I emptied a bottle of wine with him [the colonel], half asleep but in an excellent mood, I took leave of him and threw myself, after this exciting day, with a feeling of work completed into the bed that my faithful Vinke had prepared for me.)

For this private expedition he receives the *Ritterkreuz des Hausordens von Hohenzollern* (the Knight's Cross of the Family Order of the House of Hohenzollern), as well as a silver cup bearing the inscription, *Dem Sieger von Moeuvres* (To the victor of Moeuvres). During this particular attack, all the non-commissioned officers and one-third of the privates die in the enemy trenches, not to mention those who are wounded. Again, the suggestion is that *Krieg ist Krieg*, war is war.

Before the battle of the Somme, Jünger states that words like *ausweichen* (evading or fleeing) are unknown to him and his comrades. Position entrusted to them can be lost only after the last defender has died. In his subsequent actions he proves the validity of this statement. During an overpowering English attack, he forces at gun point fleeing soldiers, numbed by a day and a night of heavy drum-fire, to turn and fight again. At a later time he states, "Mit Bitten, Befehlen und Kolbenstössen schafften wir eine neue Feuerfront." (With pleadings, commands and blows of the rifles we created a new firing line.) In moments of horror, when the end of the world seems at hand, he transposes himself into a pleasant kind of intoxication by mumbling to himself a pithy saying by Ariosto, "Ein grosses Herz fühlt vor dem Tod kein Grauen, wann er auch kommt, wenn er nur rühmlich ist." (A great heart feels no terror of Death, no matter when it comes, as long as it is glorious.)

Jünger's *Der Kampf als inneres Erlebnis* appeared in 1922. Here, more than in his previous works, he depicts the odious side of the war, in a way very similar to that of Remarque. He describes repeatedly the various stages of decomposition of the dead who cannot be buried because of enemy fire:

> Manch einer zerging ohne Kreuz und Hügel in Regen, Sonne und Wind, Fliegen umschwirrten seine Einsamkeit in dichter Wolke, schwüler Dunsthauch umschwebte ihn. Unverkennbar ist der Geruch der verwesenden Menschen, schwer, süsslich und widerlich haftend wie zäher Brei. Nach grossen Schlachten brütete er so lastend über den Feldern, dass auch der Hungrigste das Essen vergass.

> (Many a soldier disintegrated without cross and mound, in rain, sun and wind. Flies buzzed round his solitude in a thick cloud. Sultry vapours hovered about him. Unmistakable is the stench of decomposing humans, heavily, sweetly and repugnantly stagnant like gluey pulp. After great battles it weighed so heavily on the fields that even the hungriest forgot to eat.)

On humid nights swollen corpses come to life again and gases escape with hissing sounds out of the wounds. To Jünger a most terrible sight is a human cadaver which continues to exist only as a crawling multitude of worms. He mentions the dead animals that hang on their chains in the barns of deserted farms, the fat rat that jumped at him while he was pulling apart a pile of corpses to find a dead friend. Yet, when Jünger sees and describes the horror of the war, he does so with great coolness, aloofness and unconcern. Moreover, in spite of all these horrid pictures that have become his life-long companions, he continues to sing the praises of the war and succumbs to its intoxications perhaps even more than in his war diaries.

With a certain effort to be fair, Jünger admits that one can be a pacifist out of idealism, that one can oppose war out of love for man. This type of pacifist he calls, with his preference for martial terminology, a soldier of the idea who, because he has courage, deserves respect. However, he feels that true conscientious objectors are not very numerous. Most pacifists, according to Jünger, are cowards, people who worship themselves, who have regard only for their own personal welfare. If the soul and the morale of a whole people drift in the direction of such selfish concerns, then the downfall of that people is at hand, though its culture be at ever so high a level. Therefore the holiest duty of the highest culture is to have the strongest fighting forces. Who and what could be holier than a fighting man, asks Jünger. Nothing, he answers, not even a god.

Although in Remarque's writings we never find a canonization of the man of courage, he by no means denies the existence of bravery. Yet there is a fundamental difference between the kind of courage that Remarque observes and that seen by Jünger. First of all he describes the desperate heroism of soldiers who, like threatened animals, are not really fighting but are rather defending themselves against annihilation. Out of love and lust for life they kill, destroy, cause havoc among those who come running across the fields with rifles, hand grenades and flame-throwers in their hands. They become heroes not because of some nebulous ideal that a rapturous schoolmaster, in the security of a classroom, has planted in them. It is a matter of killing or being killed, or of destroying so that one may live. These are the rules of conduct for the day and the basis of heroism as Remarque sees it.

Secondly, he sees the pitiful bravery of the young recruits who, barely more than children, have come directly from school to the battlefield, with only a few weeks of military training.

Die blassen Steckrübengesichter, die armselig gekrallten Hände, die jammervolle Tapferkeit dieser armen Hunde, die trotzdem vorgehen und angreifen, diese braven, armen Hunde, die so

verscüchtert sind, dass sie nicht laut zu schreien wagen und mit
zerrissenen Brüsten und Bäuchen und Armen und Beinen leise
nach ihrer Mutter wimmern und gleich aufhören, wenn man sie
ansieht!

(Their pale turnip faces, their wretchedly clenched hands, the
pitiable courage of these poor devils who, in spite of everything,
charge and attack, these brave, poor devils who are so scared that
they do not dare cry out loudly but, with lacerated chests and
bellies and arms and legs, whimper only softly for their mothers
and cease as soon as anyone looks at them.)

This deep concern for the suffering victims of the war, not only on the
German but also on the enemy side, among the French population and the
Russian prisoners, this love for one's neighbour so characteristic of Remarque,
is almost totally absent in Jünger's books about the first World War. At times
it is appalling to see Jünger's utter disregard for the hardships and horrors that
the war inflicts upon man and beast, upon soldier and civilian alike. When he
dreams his glorious dreams about "truly great men" like Alexander, Caesar,
Frederick the Great and Napoleon, he does not realize what an endless
number of men, women and children had to die an inhuman death to lay the
foundations of fame for these "truly great men"; when he pictures himself as
the prince of the trenches, when he has feelings of awe and reverence for
himself, he fails to remember the little girl lying on her face in a pool of blood
in the village of Combles, another victim of his beloved "manly courage."

While hospitals in almost every land are filled with blind and mutilated
victims of the war, while millions of children grow up fatherless and a
generation of girls remains unmarried, Jünger elaborates on his justification
of war. "Durch Krieg erst wurden grosse Religionen Gut der ganzen Erde,
schossen die tüchtigsten Rassen aus dunklen Wurzeln zum Licht, wurden
unzählige Sklaven freie Männer. Der Krieg ist ebensowenig eine
menschliche Einrichtung wie der Geschlechtstrieb; er ist ein Naturgesetz."
(Only through war did great religions become the property of the whole
world, the fittest races grow up from dark roots to the light, countless slaves
become free men. War is no more a human institution than the sex drive.
War is a law of nature.) Jünger's position is best epitomized by the refrain
from a song of the later *Hitlerjugend* (Hitler Youth), "Wir werden
weitermarschieren, / Wenn alles in Scherben fällt." (We shall march on, /
Even though everything may fall to pieces.)

Jünger's attitude is even more lamentable since he is not simply an
enraptured war reporter or a journalistic writer but a revered writer whose

works are widely read and admired. Moreover, Jünger is a writer who can claim to speak with authority about the war because he fought courageously for four long years at the focal points of the most critical engagements. On the other hand, it is not surprising that after 1945 there were voices, particularly in Eastern Germany, demanding that he be tried at Nuremberg, along with the other war criminals, as the teacher of men like Baldur von Schirach and Hans Fritzsche and as the champion of the war spirit in Germany before the second World War, although Jünger had by this time arrived at a very different point of view about the war.

Both Remarque and Jünger commit the fallacy of generalization for each portrays a certain type of soldier, basically himself, and attempts to create the impression that this type is representative of the whole army. Jünger mentions the soldiers of his battalion, who volunteer to a man to join his private expeditions and almost weep when they are not among those whom he chooses. We are led to believe that, even on the eve of the war, an overwhelming majority of the soldiers are filled with enthusiasm, devotion to their officers, and an indomitable fighting spirit. Remarque, on the other hand, does not portray a single soldier of this type. If we accept his testimony, then the army consists of people who would gladly return to their homes and leave the privilege and the glory of a *Heldentod* for someone else to achieve. And yet Jünger and Remarque are writing about the same army.

Remarque does not adhere exclusively to a defeatist point of view, just as Jünger does not picture the war solely as a splendid, knightly adventure. As Jünger pays some fleeting attention to the horrors of modern war, so Remarque does not fail to extol the one great quality that the war, in his opinion, has produced in the fighting men—comradeship. The soldiers, as he portrays them, possess not the slightest trace of *Opferbereitschaft* (self-sacrificing devotion) for the flag and the Kaiser, or the glory and honour of the state. Jünger's sublime statement, "Ueber allem Denken und Handeln stand eine schwerste Pflicht, eine höchste Ehre und ein schimmerndes Ziel: Der Tod für das Land und seine Grösse" (Above all thoughts and actions stood one most arduous duty, one highest glory and one shining goal—death for one's country and its greatness), would mean nothing to Remarque's men. Yet for their comrades they would risk almost everything. Paul Bäumer, by himself, is just a nameless soldier in a great army, a grain of sand in an endless desert, and a mere number for the planning general. But with his comrades Kropp and Kat beside him he is ready to defend this little spark of life that is his against a world that has gone berserk.

But man-devouring war smashes the barrier that stands between him and desperation. One after the other, he loses his comrades in the slaughter of the Western front. Kropp loses one leg. Müller, who had been studying for his matriculation in the midst of drumfire, dies with a shot in the stomach. Leer bleeds to death from a shattered hip. Farmer Detering, who though only about his farm and his wife, is missing one morning. His comrades hope that he has made it to Holland and safety, but he is caught by military police on his way home to his farm and his wife. Everyone knows that his desertion is due to home-sickness and a temporary lapse and that a court-martial is not impressed by such reasons. Kat is killed and finally Paul Bäumer dies also, on a beautiful, quiet day, so quiet that the army communiqué reports, "Im Westen nichts Neues" (All quiet on the Western front). The publisher of *Im Westen nichts Neues* originally demanded that Paul Bäumer should live and survive the war to make possible the appearance of a sequel, but Remarque refused to comply with this request. In his view, an ending like this would have made the book simply a story of adventures while he intended it to be an exposé and resounding denunciation of the prostration, desolation, and misery caused by the war.

* * * * * *

In *Krieg als Volksschicksal im deutschen Schrifttum* (1934), Hermann Pongs calls *Im Westen nichts Neues* a disguised act of vengeance. He groups it with a number of books which he prefers to call collectively the "Thersites" type, after the ugly and abusive soldier-demagogue in the Trojan war. In conformity with the official Nazi point of view, Pongs states that men like Remarque falsify and debase all those values for which others have given their lives—values such as home, nation, fatherland, propriety, manliness, and honour. In their place the "Thersites" writers exalt their own atrophied egos. After elaborating this point, Pongs concludes: "Erst heute erkennt man ganz die unbewusste Rachsucht des ohne Vorbild und Auftrieb von der Schulbank in den Krieg Geworfenen und Verbeogenen, der sich das Gewicht einer ganzen Generation anmasst." (Only today does one fully realize the unconscious vindictiveness of this distorted man, who, without an ideal or inspiration, is thrown from the school bench into the war and presumptuously assumes for himself the importance of a whole generation.)

Pongs does not exactly specify against whom the alleged vindictiveness in Remarque's book is directed. A more specific and even more severe criticism is expressed by William K. Pfeiler in his book, *War and the German Mind*. He states "Individual incidents are given typical significance, less by an abstract process than by the exclusiveness with which they are presented. Thus the reader gets the impression that all officers are brutes; all teachers are cowardly shirkers who let others do the bloody and dangerous job of fighting for Germany's glory while they stay safely at home; and all doctors are inhuman monsters." Pfeiler reads a good deal into Remarque's book because such generalizations are neither expressed nor implied. In fact, Remarque even says, "Es mag gute Aerzte geben, und viele sind es; doch einmal fällt bei den hundert Untersuchungen jeder Soldat einem dieser zahlreichen Heldengreifer in die Finger. . . . " (There may be good doctors, and many are good. Nevertheless every soldier at some time during his hundreds of check-ups falls into the clutches of one of those numerous hero-hunters. . . .)

Remarque certainly entertains no thoughts of resentment against his officers, as Theodor Plievier does in *Des Kaisers Kulis*. In two instances, once in the barracks and the second time on the front, a young lieutenant takes sides with the soldiers to protect them against the affronts and molestations of Corporal Himmelstoss. The few commissioned officers that are mentioned in *Im Westen nichts Neues* are, without exception, understanding and brave men. In *Der Weg zurück*, the sequel of *Im Westen nichts Neues*, Remarque even goes a step further. He mentions the company commander, Heel, who risks his own life to rescue a wounded soldier. This is the same Heel who, alone in his office, puts his head into his hands and cries upon hearing of the Emperor's flight and upon the prospect of exchanging his officer's uniform for a private's uniform, the same Heel who is unable to speak when he wishes to say farewell to his soldiers. Remarque also refers approvingly to the discharged soldiers defending their wounded Lieutenant Breyer against a gang of Communist revolutionaries.

There is a series of accusations against the older generations for not having prevented the war, but none of them could be called vindictive. It is true that the soldiers avenge themselves on Corporal Himmelstoss for their humiliations, but these are single incidents with little bearing on the general impression that the book as a whole creates. It seems, therefore, that there is little or no justification for either Pfeiler's or Pongs' judgment, at least as far as *Im Westen nichts Neues*, the book to which they directly refer, is concerned.

Pfeiler's criticism, of course, should by no means be placed on the same level as that of Pongs, who simply indulges in biased defamations when talking about antiwar writers like Remarque. Pfeiler states: "Remarque is an artist. By his impressionistic talent he knows how to draw characters and situations that engage attention and arouse deepest sympathy. His language is versatile and concise; his narrative is rich in contrast of situations and reflections, and his composition is done with a brilliant stage technique." And yet Pfeiler, who in his preface mentions that Pongs' investigations have been of greatest value to him, seems to entertain a definite preference for books that extol duty, honour, manly deeds and sacrificial death. About Remarque's book he concludes: "Rather it is symptomatic of an age that saw the final revelation of the war in the adolescent self-pity, resentment, and sentimentality the novel embodies. Really it is the story of an egocentric, immature youngster of whom one may well wonder how he would have developed without the war. There is, indeed, plenty of authority for holding that the war helped many to find themselves and prove their mettle, and that it also exposed the brittle human substance that might have been broken by life anyway, without ever having been exposed to the destructive shells of the war."

* * * * * *

In contrast to poets such as Ernst Lissauer, who wrote a fervid, high-pitched "Hassgesang gegen England" (song of hate against England), neither Jünger nor Remarque ever shows any trace of hatred for the enemy, in spite of the waves of hostile feelings skillfully created by war propagandists in all the belligerent countries. Both display, for very different reasons, a certain amount of respectful approbation of the soldiers in the enemy trenches.

In Remarque's book this esteem grows mainly out of the author's awareness that the French soldier is a human being like himself, with the same hopes and fears. This attitude is dramatically shown when Paul Bäumer, out of fear for his own life, stabs a Frenchman who, like himself, seeks cover in a muddy shell-hole close to the French lines. Because of the proximity of the French, Paul must stay a whole day with his victim in the safety of the shell-hole. In the dead man's wallet he finds letters that he endeavours to read and some small photographs of a woman and a little girl. He also finds the soldier's name, Gérard Duval. Exhausted by hunger, thirst and lack of sleep, dejected by the silence and the presence of the dead Frenchman, he feels compelled to speak to the corpse and to ask for forgiveness.

Jünger's respect for the enemy stems from quite different feelings. While he, a man of the front, looks down with contempt and disdain on the base wallahs of the home front, he feels certain intimate connections with the fighting enemy, the simple front-line soldier, the "cochon de front." Only courage is respected by courage! He is grateful for having this dashing, reckless French neighbour who, every half century, wipes the rust off the German swords. Europe, as a peaceful, rolling country, green and pastured, with as many gregarious, good-natured animals feeding on it as it can possibly maintain, this Europe that, in Schiller's *Wallenstein*, was the dream and the ideal of the young Piccolomini, is called by Jünger a *Kelch*, an ordeal that we should be spared. He is confident that, as long as Germanic and Gallic blood flows, Europe will not sink into this lamentable condition. The full realization of the enemy's value and culture gives him a chivalrous enjoyment of a peculiar kind. Jünger is refined. He does not want to fight against barbarians. After he has stormed an enemy trench and massacred the defenders, he likes to sit down in a dug-out and read what he finds in the luggage of a French officer, something by Racine or Baudelaire.

Junger in his aristocratic vitalism extends his scorn of the home front to German civilian life as well. Equality and the mass have become the new gods, he contemptuously asserts. The current view, he feels, is that since the mass cannot become like the selected few, the selected few are expected to become like the mass. He sees the mass as a beast with a thousand heads, an envious, vulgar, base monster. Since life is hard, the multitude prefers to escape from reality into the world of the cinema. The film hero replaces true heroism, and the bourgeois, comfortably relaxing in an upholstered chair, enjoys foreign countries and wild adventures in the very heart of the big city. This thin veneer of so-called culture he finds repugnant and annoying to the innermost feelings of the true warrior. He prefers times that were more cruel, and in his book, *Der Kamp als inneres Erlebnis* he makes this point:

> Wenn asiatische Despoten, wenn ein Tamerlan das klirrende Gewölk seiner Horden über weite Länder trieb, lag vor ihnen Feuer, Wüste im Rücken. Die Bewohner riesiger Städte wurden lebendig begraben oder blutige Schädel zu Pyramiden gehäuft. Mit grosser Leidenschaft wurde geplündert, geschändet, gesengt und gesotten.
>
> Trotzdem: diese grossen Würger sind sympathischer. Sie handleten, wie es ihrem Wesen entsprach. Töten war ihnen Moral, wie den Christen Nächstenliebe. Sie waren wilde Eroberer, doch ebenso geschlossen und rund in ihrer Erscheinung wie die Hellenen in der ihren. Man kann Genuss an ihnen empfinden wie an bunten Raubtieren, die mit kühnen Lichtern in den Augen durch tropische Dichtungen brechen.

> (When Asiatic despots, when a Tamerlane drove the clattering clouds of his hordes over extensive countries, fire lay before them and desert at their rear. The inhabitants of huge cites were buried alive and bloody heads were heaped up like pyramids. They pillaged, ravished, burned and boiled with a deep passion. Notwithstanding, these great destroyers are more congenial. They acted in accordance with their character. Killing was their ethic as love of one's neighbour is the Christians' ethic. They were wild conquerors but were also as well-rounded and consistent in their appearance as the Hellenes in theirs. One can enjoy them as colourful beasts of prey which break through tropical thickets with daring lights in their eyes.)

The goddess Fortuna has poured out of her cornucopia such a profusion and superabundance of favours and gifts over Lieutenant Jünger that he loses all solid ground from under his feet. He reaches the climax and the most extreme of his position when he justifies war as an end in itself. Not for what we fight, but how we fight, is the most important consideration. War is sanctified by a cause, but a cause is even more sanctified by war. And even the soldier who fights for an unjust cause does not fight in vain. "Leben heisst töten" (to live means to kill).

Eugen Gürster-Steinhausen, in his essay "Ernst Jünger—der Prophet des deutschen Nationalismus," maintains that the *Dichter* Jünger, as nobody before him, exhausts the possibilities of the German language in an attempt to immunize the German youth against the horrors of coming wars. The view that Jünger exhausts the possibilities of the German language is of course a little extreme. Gürster-Steinhausen shows convincingly that many of Jünger's apodictic statements and philosophical ideas are merely new versions of some glittering Nietzschean epigrams. He sees as the basic difference between Nietzsche's *Übermensch* and Jünger's revolutionary nationalist and heroic nihilist the fact that Nietzsche advocated beast-of-prey instincts during a time of relative security, while the latter preached his merciless tidings when beasts of prey were already roaming about freely. Gürster-Steinhausen also calls attention to the striking similarity between Hitler's and Jünger's writings.

* * * * * *

Interesting points of comparison are the style, the language and the use of humour employed by Jünger and Remarque. While Jünger's prose is sober, restrained, disciplined and yet supple, energetic and vigorous, Remarque's language is multifarious and colourful in its abundance of contrasts and, especially toward the end, full of resignation. While Jünger describes the war, which he calls a natural phenomenon, objectively and from a cool and lofty height and in civilized, clear-cut terms, Remarque oscillates from idyllic, emotional, tender and delicate passages to coarse, lurid, and at times shocking, risqué descriptions. Indeed this harshness, this crudity, occasionally reaches proportions that necessitated alterations in the original English translations to insure that the book could be mailed in the United States, in conformity with the federal and state laws governing obscene literature.

In spite of the drab pictures that Remarque paints of the war itself, there are several instances of racy, pithy, down-to-earth humour in his book. When he mentions, for example, that the poor and simple people considered the war a calamity from the very beginning, while the so-called upper-class people had revelled in it, although they should have been more aware of the implications, he says, "Katczinsky behauptet, das käme von der Bildung, sie mache dämlich. Und was Kat sagt, das hat er sich überlegt." (Katczinsky maintains that they were like that because of their education, which makes people dull. And what Kat says, he has thought over.) Some effective ribald persiflage is seen in the passage about the soldiers settling accounts with Corporal Himmelstoss and later with the former teacher Kantorek, although William K. Pfeiler asserts concerning this incident with Kantorek, "This particular scene, told with the malicious glee of an adolescent is typical of the immature and sophomoric attitude of the heroes."

Humour is virtually absent in Jünger's writings about the first World War. There is a passage which contains what he calls a "certain bloody humour." A stutterer returning from a patrol is shot at and wounded because he cannot respond quickly enough to the demand for the password. An intoxicated soldier climbs over the trenches and conducts a private rifle-fire against his own comrades until they pull him in and give him a sound beating. The grimly "humorous" stories that he hears from the French in Cambrais during a furlough are of a similar type.

Stephen Leacock, in his essay "Humour as I see it," considers this particular type of humour suitable only for savages or prehistoric men who, after watching a skater describing graceful circles on the ice and then seeing him break through never to come up again, stand around the ice-hole laughing until their sides have split. If we accept Leacock's definition that it is the essence and prime condition of good humour "that it must be without harm or malice, nor should it convey even incidentally any real picture of sorrow or suffering or death," then Jünger's books about the first World War contain no humour whatsoever.

* * * * * *

Neither Jünger nor Remarque sees any eternal values, *Ewigkeitswerte* (a term used by Remarque), in his works on the first World War; both are well aware that their works, from a literary point of view, are not above criticism. Jünger, with his war diaries, considers himself to be doing only preparatory work for the coming great *Dichter* who will write an epic comparable to the *Nibelungenlied*. When referring to himself, Jünger always employs the word *Autor* rather than *Dichter*. In spite of the fact that he laid the foundation of his fame with his works on the first World War they are of a decidedly youthful and provisional character. Similarly Remarque, despite the great success of his novels, is very modest concerning their literary merits. In an interview in 1946 he says about *Im Westen nichts Neues*, "It was simply a collection of the best stories that I told and my friends told as we sat over drinks and relived the war." A responsible critic, Arthur Eloesser, has called *Im Westen nichts Neues* "a brilliant piece of journalism, raised to the level of art by accepting the limitations of sobriety."

Der Weg zurück presents a somewhat different picture. Like *Im Westen nichts Neues*, it is a semi-autobiographical work. It opens with a prologue depicting life on the battlefields of France during the last weeks of the war. It describes the retreat of the soldiers after Armistice Day, and finally the difficulties and hardships that lay in wait for them at home. The heroes of this novel are survivors of the group portrayed in *Im Westen nichts Neues*. There are also occasional references to the dead comrades: Paul Bäumer, Stanislaus Katczinsky, Detering, Paul Kemmerich and Leer. *Der Weg zurück* is a good piece of narrative but there are some passages that betray the fact that the author has resorted to routine work. Some of the themes of *Im Westen nichts Neues*, very effective in the first novel because of their conciseness, are reintroduced, but they are no longer effective. The former sniper, in contrast to the man who is haunted day and night by the shadows of the enemies he has killed, is rather overdrawn in his proud recounting of all the foes that he has disposed of with his skill as a sharp-shooter; both figures appear already in *Im Westen nichts Neues*. The retaliation against the former sergeant-major, Seelig, for his baseness on the front is all but too reminiscent of that taken by the soldiers against Corporal Himmelstoss without, however, approaching the comic quality and ludicrousness of that episode. Even the idyllic or pastoral passages in *Im Westen nichts Neues* reappear, this time in a barren, stereotyped form, while the lurid realism has been intensified to the point where it almost becomes vulgar and obscene.

The plight of the disbanded soldiers who are unable to adjust and acclimatize themselves arouses the reader's sympathy and compassion. Yet in several incidents they behave like ruffians and bullies who intimidate their fellow citizens by threats and actual physical violence, although, of course, they do so because of their helplessness and their inability to cope with the multitude of problems that confront them at home. After they spend their youth in the trenches of the Western front and escape death only by chance, they return full of hope to the land for which they fought, only to discover that they have become superfluous, an unnecessary surplus in whom hardly anybody is interested.

Der weg zurück also contains a few passages that reveal Remarque's belief that all the suffering has not been entirely in vain, but will bear fruit on some far-off day. George Rahe, the former lieutenant who has been unable to find the road back into civilian life, finally returns to the barren fields of battle in France where he spent his youth. He can still detect the old odour of blood, powder, and earth. He walks through the trenches and the shell-holes, past ammunition pouches and hand-grenades covered with mud, past bits of a belt and pieces of grey-green cloth—the remains of a soldier. And finally he stands in front of the long rows of black crosses. Here lie buried the lost years that found no fulfillment and the strength and will of a generation that died before it had begun to live. His hand goes to his pocket and back to his head and a shot rings out over the former battlefield. He falls to his knees and with one final effort he raises himself to see the crosses marching to fight their last battle, the battle for life and peace. Peter Hagboldt writes somewhat rhapsodically about this passage, "Hope in the future is expressed most beautifully and poetically in an unforgettable scene in Remarque, in which George Rahe, a man broken by the war, kills himself after the armistice, a victim of both—war and peace."

* * * * * *

Both Jünger and Remarque, in their novels on World War I, try to give a faithful and valid picture of the same theatre of the war, the Western front, but their works show little similarity. Jünger succeeds in portraying the heroism and the intoxication that the experience of the battle stimulates in the soldier. Some passages in his diaries and essays are fascinating reading. They show "the great force and economy of his writing. . . . his avoidance of false heroism, and his ability to express something of the tremendous and shattering impact of the experience." His unreserved glorification of war and his lack of any humane feelings for the innocent victims of war are, however, somewhat shocking to the modern reader. Remarque's books, on the other hand, are impressive protests against war and the sufferings produced by war. They do not contain the exciting reproductions of single incidents of battle that we find in Jünger's works, nor are they written in the energetic, vigorous style of *In Stahlgewittern*. The language of Remarque's novels on World War I is concise and yet versatile and multifarious. In structure, they are series of episodes skillfully held together by the protagonist who tells the story in the first person. Neither Jünger's nor Remarque's writings on the first World War present a balanced or unbiased picture of the Western front. They are not objective reporting but subjective and highly selective accounts. Only when we allow the works of one author to complement those of the other can we arrive at a true picture of the German soldier in World War I.

A. F. BANCE

Im Westen nichts Neues:
A Bestseller in Context

It fell to Erich Maria Remarque, born Erich Paul Remark, to write the best-known war book to emerge from the First World War in any country. *Im Westen nichts Neues* also represents a unique publishing event. And yet, perhaps because of its phenomenal commercial success, it has received relatively little serious discussion. No one would want to claim for the novel a place in the ranks of first-class literature, but nonetheless a work so powerful in its effects deserves some appraisal. Seen in the context of its time, as an expression of Weimar Germany and as the popular European war-book *par excellence*, it is an intriguing subject still. The reasons for its success, both domestic and foreign, are not the least part of the book's interest for us today.

Im Westen nichts Neues appeared in the *Vossische Zeitung* as a serial from 10 November to 9 December 1928, and was issued in book form by the Propyläenverlag on 31 January 1929. Its initial domestic success might be thought to be adequately explained by publicity. The house of Ullstein laid on a sales campaign unprecedented for the time, enormous numbers of review copies being sent out and all the resources of the great publishing house put at Remarque's disposal. Within twelve weeks of its appearance, its German sales had already reached half a million copies, and by then it had been translated into fourteen languages. Within a year of publication the figure of a million sales in Germany alone had been achieved. The intensive

From *The Modern Language Review*. © 1977 Modern Humanities Research Association.

sales campaign did not slacken: the first two thousand of the second million of the German edition were printed in Braille, and presented to blinded ex-soldiers in May 1930. By this time the number of translations had risen to twenty-three, and the total circulation, excluding pirated editions produced in Soviet Russia, Turkey, Yugoslavia, and China, was estimated to have reached three million. The Italian version was banned by Mussolini. The film version which quickly followed publication obviously did nothing to harm sales, especially as the première in December 1930 was turned into the occasion for a curiously juvenile set-piece demonstration by the Nazis, who 'under Goebbels's leadership, led riots against the film, invaded the theatre, throwing stink bombs and letting loose mice, and finally succeeded in having the film banned' (Peter Gay, *Weimar Culture* (London, 1969)). The notoriety of the novel was a publisher's delight, and Remarque, intentionally or not, seems to have aided it by playing the part of the mystery man. He declared that he had written *Im Westen* in order to free his mind from an oppression; that he never imagined it would become famous; that he would not discuss it or supervise the filming of the story; and that he might never write again. An anti-Remarque industry sprang up in the wake of the novel. In 1930 one Peter Kropp wrote a book entitled *Endlich Klarheit über Remarque und sein Buch 'Im Westen nichts Neues'* (Hamm, Westf.), and Emil Marius Requark sold twenty thousand copies of his reputedly feeble skit *Vor Troja nichts Neues* (Berlin, 1930). No doubt all this, too, was grist to the publicity mill.

Remarque certainly shows all the popular novelist's facility for smoothing the reader's path, in this case by means of a setting evoked with sufficient realism, yet not stretching the reader's imagination too much; a varied pace created by stirring events alternating with restful periods of calm (as the story progresses to its climax, action dominates increasingly); and certain easily-recognized stereotype characters. But commercial luck and acumen do not exclusively account for the success of Remarque's novel. Apart from any intrinsic merits it may have, the date of its appearance played an important part. In 1928 nearly all nations officially renounced war through the Kellogg-Briand Peace Pact. Anti-war sentiment had reached its climax. At the same time there was a tide in the psychological affairs of men that brought a renewal of interest in the Great War. The public was ready to read about it, and writers to respond. Although the legend of 'die Verspätung der Kriegsliteratur' has now been substantially revised, it is true to say that it was not until a decade after the end of the fighting that many writers, with a strange unanimity, began to turn their war experience into literary form. After 1927 an international crop of war books appeared. In defeated Germany it was, on the whole and for complex reasons, the writers of a pacifist disposition who were slower to make their mark. The successful early war books (e.g. those of Walter Flex and Ernst Jünger) had been predominantly 'heroic' or militarist in outlook, in contrast to the pacifism of, for example, the best-known early French products such as *Les Croix de Bois* by Roland Dorgelès (1919) and Barbusse's *Le Feu* (1916). But by 1927 the balance began to be redressed in Germany. Although war books of the Right continued to appear (and may even have received some impetus from works like *Im Westen nichts Neues*), the more pacifist novel came into its own, with Arnold Zweig's *Der Streit um den Sergeanten Grisha* (1927), Ludwig Renn's *Krieg* (1928), *Im Westen* in 1929, Theodor Plievier's *Des Kaisers Kulis* and Edlef Köppen's *Heeresbericht* (1930).

Remarque's statement that he only wrote *Im Westen* in order to free himself from an obsession has a familiar ring. There is probably little reason to doubt its sincerity. So many writers struggled ten years to assimilate the war experience, and the phenomenon is one that ignores frontiers. Richard Aldington in the dedication to his *Death of a Hero* (London, 1929) reports that he began the novel immediately after the Armistice, while he was still in Belgium, but that he 'threw it aside, and never picked it up again.' He goes on to say: 'The attempt was premature. Then, ten years later, almost day for day, I felt the impulse return, and began this book.' The preface to Edmund Blunden's *Undertones of War* (London, 1928) tells a similar tale: 'I tried once before. . . . But what I then wrote. . . . was noisy with a depressing forced gaiety then very much the rage.'

One characteristic which distinguishes Remarque's novel from the rest is the thoroughness with which he assimilated his war-obsession to fictional form. Robert Graves's experience is probably more typical. According to *Goodbye to All That* (London, 1929) Graves was haunted by daydreams of the trenches until well into 1928, and when he did write his war-book he was unable to find a fictional medium that did not seem to him a betrayal of the truth:

> I made several attempts during these years to rid myself of the poison of war memories by finishing my novel, but I had to abandon them . . . ashamed at having distorted my material with a plot, yet not sure enough of myself to retranslate it into undisguised history.

Graves's difficulty in finding the right fictional form for a war-book illuminates the general problem of achieving sufficient distance from experience to produce ambitious fiction, and the guilt that is associated with the attempt to do so. Almost universally, the need to wring from the war a clear moral message seems to conflict with the demands of fiction. Remarque stepped in where angels feared to tread. The time was ripe for a pacifist war-book and the public was clearly grateful for the simple fictional form he created.

For *Im Westen* is undeniably fiction. The novel is not autobiographical to any marked degree, and it is remarkably free from the obligation to the documentary that is common to most war-books. Dates and places are hardly mentioned. The war does not fall into individual battles (Verdun, the Somme) but is a continuous undifferentiated process, like a conveyor belt. There is no indication of a strategic awareness of the hostilities as a whole, and no analysis of the causes or deeper significance of the war as a historical event, such as can be found in almost any other war-book. These very limitations, we would suggest, have contributed to the novel's lasting success and universal appeal.

Remarque capitalizes on the bare *Fronterlebnis*, for the authenticity which this experience lends his novel needs no further embellishment. There is an interesting parallel with the way that Hitler's speeches and career capitalized on his front line experience as the ultimate legitimation of his message, superseding politics, for: 'are not feelings, unlike the complexities of economics or politics, something Everyman can understand and judge and share?' In these terms, lack of documentation means a *greater* authenticity in the novel, not less, and paradoxically the documentary obsession of other war-writers can be seen simply as obscuring the authenticity of their personal statements. There is very little in *Im Westen* to inhibit the reader's response; the lowest common denominator is invariably found. Paul Bäumer, the hero, though not lacking in educational background (and the conventional artistic aspirations of the *Abiturient*) deliberately assumes and even exaggerates the ignorance of the humblest ranker. Remarque reduces him totally to the passive object of official decisions. There is a great deal of popular attraction, as well as some truth, in the view of the war as a social leveller. In the front line, education and class confer few advantages. There are not many other successful works which exploit this aspect of the war so thoroughly.

Among the list of well-known war-books given by George Orwell in 'Inside the Whale' we find none which adheres so strictly to the limited point of view of the private soldier as *Im Westen*. The *poilus* in *Le Feu* are infinitely more sophisticated than Paul Bäumer and his friends, and have only too clear an insight into their situation. The British or American novels that Orwell mentions are written by or about officers or combatants who are officer-material (Hemingway's *A Farewell to Arms*, Graves's *Goodbye to All That*, Sassoon's *Memoirs of an Infantry Officer*, and *A Subaltern on the Somme* by 'Mark VII,' i.e. Mark Plowman). In comparison with other German war-books, too, Remarque's vision is severely reduced. Certainly this does not preclude discussion of the war and war-aims among his soldiers (whereas in the British books, by contrast with the continental ones, such general discussions are comparatively rare). But the discussion is vague and ill-informed, and amounts to little more than grumbling between offensives. Its naïveté emphasizes the helplessness of the serving man.

It may well be that the undocumentary vagueness that characterizes *Im Westen*, the reduction of vision to the immediate moment, was favourably received in 1929 because the essential aspects of the war which it conveys correspond quite closely to the surviving European folk-memory for trench warfare. In other words, *Im Westen* was the Great War *comme il faut*.

The structure makes few demands; it is an episodic series of anecdotes typifying the experience of the war generation as Remarque sees it: from school to basic training; the first taste of the front with a working party; the retreat to the rear; the front line again in all its horrors; the comic relief behind the lines when the hero and friends make their conquest of some local ladies; going on leave; the return to the front; being wounded, convalescent, and sent back to the fighting again; the increasing despair, apathy and perverse pride of the veteran, etc. Remarque knows how to emphasize by selection: we learn surprisingly little in detail about life in the trenches. As Pfeiler pointed out, 'in a book which claims to be a report of the front by a front soldier, of 288 pages of text only about 80 pages deal with situations at or right behind the front, and even they are heavily interspersed with reflections.' Strong emphasis is therefore thrown on to those aspects of the front which *are* mentioned, and from a documentary point of view certain exciting elements of 1914–18 warfare are dramatized unduly. There is the apparent frequency of the attacks (when much of front-line life consisted in reality of tedious and uncomfortable inactivity, with the occasional patrol into no-man's-land or raid on enemy lines); there is hand-to-hand combat and the sight of the enemy dying slowly at your hands, in contrast to the dealing of death at long distance which was much more typical of the war. There are the fits of berserk blood-lust that descend upon the attacker during an offensive. None of the war-books avoid horrors, but Remarque heaps them up unmercifully. He is given to sensational touches and macabre effects to intensify the horrors of war: the screaming of the wounded horses is a sentimental and gruesome motif that became a feature of many a war-novel after *Im Westen*. The first full-length description of action sets the scene in a churchyard where the hero cowers beneath a heavy artillery bombardment combined with a gas attack, while coffins fly through the air around him. The elimination of each member of the small group of comrades by turn, until only the hero is left, is a conventional but effective technique, and the death of Bäumer at the eleventh hour, in the last days of

October 1918, after he has survived the worst years of the war, is a somewhat sensational and contrived, though not impossible, dénouement. The breach of narratorial discipline involved in the abrupt and unexplained change from the first person perspective and from historic present to the past tense in the final short paragraph, following Bäumer's death, is in keeping with the unselfconscious presentation of the story throughout.

Yet the book's limited vision is effective, taken on its own terms. For example, the strongly developed sense of living in the moment and the blurring of the passage of time in the trenches reflect the dehumanizing effect of a war which turned the ordinary soldier into an automaton, a part of the war-machine:

> Vergehen Wochen—Monate—Jahre? Es sind nur Tage. Wir sehen die Zeit neben uns schwinden in den farblosen Gesichtern der Sterbenden, wir löffeln Nahrung in uns hinein, wir laufen, wir werfen, wir schießen, wir töten, wir liegen herum, wir sind schwach und stumpf . . .

It suits Remarque to depict his heroes as 'puny creatures at the mercy of inhuman technology.' The point becomes clear if we compare almost any other war-books and the relative sovereignty of their heroes. For officers on both sides, relief from the front was much easier to achieve than for other ranks (although, of course, the casualty rate among officers was much higher). It is not surprising then to find that in the British books the hero still has to some degree a sense of being master of his own fate. The same holds true for Jünger in *In Stahlgewittern*. But the sharpness of this contrast signifies more than a mere discussion of rank: it reminds us that *Im Westen* is a novel of Weimar Germany. Commentators have noted that in the last years of Weimar the individual became fully aware of his limited freedom of action in the face of social, industrial and political forces. Egon Schwarz sees the expression of this loss of identity as the chief function of *Neue Sachlichkeit* literature, namely 'das Augenmerk auf jene gigantischen und doch im Verborgenen wirkenden Kräfte zu richten, denen gegenüber die Bewegungsfreiheit des Einzelnen zu einer *quantité négligeable* zusammengeschrumpft war.' The war in its later phase, the *Materialschlacht*, is highly symbolic of the mass industrial age voraciously devouring men and materials in a self-perpetuating system.

In *Im Westen* this statement is always implicit, however, never enshrined in formal political utterances which might deter the reader. The characters of *Im Westen*, like so many created by the pacifist wing of *Neue Sachlichkeit*, are apolitical. The novel presents a very generalized pacifism, not a detailed programme but something akin to a pious wish for international amity, unlikely to arouse much resistance. Even then, the pacifism is diluted (certainly when compared to *Le Feu*!). After spending a night of profound penitence pinned down in a shell crater with the body of the Frenchman he has killed in hand-to-hand combat, Bäumer makes the dead man a promise he knows even at the time he cannot keep:

> Aber wenn ich davonkomme, Kamerad, will ich kämpfen gegen dieses, das uns beide zerschlug: dir das Leben—und mir—? Auch das Leben. Ich verspreche es dir, Kamerad. Es darf nie wieder geschehen.

These thoughts, like a reversion to prayer in moments of danger, can be dismissed when "normal" conditions are resumed.

Bäumer is kind to the Russian prisoners of war in his charge, and at one point his thoughts dwell on the process by which international treaties artificially create hostility between private citizens of different nations who bear each other no personal grudge. But the front line is no place for such thoughts and they are banished to the margin for the duration: 'hier darf ich nicht weiterdenken. Dieser Weg geht in den Abgrund.' No doubt the implication is that the 1929 reader should be taking up this cause. Such pacifism seems today utterly banal. The emotional appeal is simple and commits no one to action or the sacrifice of his personal interests. It even exists comfortably alongside the thrill of battle, the pride of the veteran soldier, and the assertion of Germany's undefeated military efficiency: 'wir sind nicht geschlagen, denn wir sind als Soldaten besser und erfahrener.' For many Germans in 1929, this must have offered a very acceptable package to fill (however momentarily) the moral vacuum experienced by the Weimar generation. The message is delivered with a fervency which contrasts with its innocuous content:

> Mein Herz klopft: ist hier das Ziel, das Große, das Einmalige, an das ich im Graben gedacht habe, das ich suchte als Daseinsmöglichkeit nach dieser Katastrophe aller Menschlichkeit, ist es eine Aufgabe für das Leben nachher, würdig der Jahre des Grauens?

The very modesty of Remarque's pacifism, such as it is, is highly appropriate to the nature of Weimar society, which, for all its cultural and artistic ferment, had in the main few ambitions in the direction of radical reform, and sought security rather than political revolution.

In the same way that Remarque discovers a formula that promises the least possible resistance to the idealistic content of his novel, so does he attempt to represent the fate of a whole generation through characters whose individuality is minimal. Jost Hermand has rightly remarked that Paul Bäumer is 'eine genau durchdachte Typisierung' who, despite the apparently individualized treatment, has no 'psychologisch erfaßbare Privaterlebnisse' (*Die sogenannten zwanziger Jahre*). He is the Everyman subsumed in the first person plural of Erich Kästner's poem on the lost generation, 'Jahrgang 1899' (Remarque was born in 1898):

> Wir haben der Welt in die Schnauze geguckt,
> anstatt mit Puppen zu spielen.
> Wir haben der Welt auf die Weste gespuckt,
> soweit wir vor Ypern nicht fielen
>
> Man hat unsern Körper und hat unsern Geist
> ein wenig zu wenig gekräftigt.
> Man hat uns zu lange, zu früh und zumeist
> mit der Weltgeschichte beschäftigt!

Pfeiler points out that the factual evidence (the war-letters of students, the work of Walter Flex, etc.) shows that Remarque's heroes are not truly representative of a whole generation, but only of a certain type. But what may not be quite true of the war generation may be more appropriate to Weimar Germany, its despair and loss of direction. Remarque's tendency to claim homogeneity for his generation conforms to the well-known collectivism, 'der Zug ins Kollektivierende' (*Die sogenannten zwanziger Jahre*) that characterizes Weimar Germany and its literature which, in the latter phase, tends towards the panoramic reflection of mass culture. (Examples are war-novels like Arnold Zweig's *Der Striet um den Sergeanten Grischa*, and Ludwig Renn's *Krieg*; factory-novels like Erik Reger's *Union der festen Hand* (1931); metropolitan novels like Döblin's *Berlin Alexanderplatz* (1929); novels of the Depression like Leonhard Frank's *Von drei Millionen drei* (1932), etc.) By contrast, the society that is reflected in the British war-books—both that of 1914–18 and that of the late twenties and thirties—is clearly intact and unified to a degree unknown in Weimar Germany. For that reason, the heroes are too individualistic and too wrapped up in the intensity of their own private experience to consider themselves as part of a collective called a 'generation.'

Remarque's generation is the one that was just old enough at the beginning of the war to go straight from school into the trenches. Its experience, Remarque claims, is more shattering, its fate more pathetic than that of others slightly older or slightly younger (the former had already established the basis of an existence before the war, the latter escaped the same total exposure to it). In other war novels, characters are revealed, and perhaps warped, but not, as in *Im Westen*, entirely formed by the war situation. For Remarque's youngsters the war is a total experience, it is *the* experience (again we are reminded of Hitler's speeches) which imprints itself on a *tabula rasa*. War becomes the only point of reference in a world that is otherwise totally incomprehensible. This sensational and monumental totality may be another source of the appeal of *Im Westen*. But it is interesting to speculate also what part of its appeal, in Germany at any rate, was due to its continuation of the theme of rebellion of the school-pupil against a rigid and despotic, but essentially hollow caste of pedagogues. Wedekind's *Frühlings Erwachen* or Robert Musil's *Törless*, Thomas Mann's *Buddenbrooks* or Heinrich Mann's *Professor Unrat* reveal the moral bankruptcy which the German pedagogue disguised in a zealous rectitude. There is a whole generation of *Schulromane* contemporary with *Im Westen*, such as Walter Harich's *Die Primaner* (1931), Franz Werfel's *Abituriententag*, Ernst Glaeser's *Jahrgang 1902* (1928), and Friedrich Torberg's *Der Schüler Gerber hat absolviert* (1930), which explore the betrayal of the 'lost generation' by its elders. The picture of the educational failure of the pre-war German schools that emerges is a dual one: on the one hand the pupil was overburdened by the sheer weight of subject-matter, so that the problem of examinations assumed monstrous proportions; on the other, despite lip-service to a fine old tradition of *Bildung*, German schools were austere places of instruction rather than of education in the wider English sense, and the efficient Prussian autocracy of the Hohenzollerns gave rise to the conception of an efficient citizen-subject, well instructed, obedient, trustworthy, and a loyal instrument of the state.

In *Im Westen* the old culture collapses at the first shot: 'Das erste Trommelfeuer zeigte uns unseren Irrtum, und unter ihm stürzte die Weltanschauung zusammen, die sie uns gelehrt hatten.' If we compare the British war-books we see that the manly, anti-intellectual and games-centred ethos of the English public school could be transferred with great ease to the front-line situation. There is a verse by R. E. Vernède which neatly expresses the point:

> Lad, with the merry smile and the eyes
>> Quick as a hawk's and clear as the day,
> You who have counted the game the prize,
>> Here is the game of games to play.

> Never a goal—the captains say—
> Matches the one that's needed now:
> Put the old blazer and cap away—
> England's colours await your brow.

One public-school quality in particular, the phlegmatic self-control implied in the understatement of Blunden's title, *Undertones of War*, was undoubtedly useful in a static war of attrition.

German *Bildung* (as reflected in *Im Westen* and other works) is more pretentious in its claims, based on precept rather than example, divorced from everyday practicality, and (in the worst sense) idealized. In *Im Westen* the effect of a brutal confrontation with the realty of warfare is that all established values are immediately wiped out. *Bildung*, with its strong insistence on respect for authority, is revealed as a preparation for slaughter. The adolescents reply by creating a kind of alternative society. Moral law is rewritten on the battlefield. If a badly wounded man is going to die in any case and is suffering unbearable agony, the question is whether one is justified in shooting him for mercy's sake, and the answer is yes (though it remains a hypothetical answer). The old rules are now irrelevant, like the academic education of the pre-war German schools. Other rules are developed, such as that which forbids a saw edge on one's bayonet, for fear of an unpleasant death at the hands of the enemy if one is captured. A new practical education for survival is required, like a grotesque parody of Baden-Powell's *Scouting for Boys*: you must not only know how to light a fire with wet wood, but also how to stick the enemy with your bayonet without getting it irretrievably fixed.

Despite the pacifist message, much of this must inevitably contain a certain glamour for the youthful mind. By the same token, much of the novel exploits the attractions of a juvenile rude gesture to the adult world. The greatest bliss behind the lines is a communal visit to the latrines in one-man open cabins drawn into a sociable circle. 'Dem Soldaten ist sein Magen und seine Verdauung ein vertrauteres Gebeit als jedem anderen Menschen. Dreiviertel seines Wortschatzes sind ihm entnommen . . . Unsere Familien und unsere Lehrer werden sich schön wundern, wenn wir nach Hause kommen. . . .' Nothing is more important than eating, drinking, and sleeping. It was long ago pointed out that there is a good deal of juvenile wish-fulfillment in *Im Westen*. The revulsion against authority is concentrated on two symbolic figures, the schoolmaster Kantorek, who patriotically inspires his whole class to enlist, an Corporal Himmelstoss, a postman in civilian life, who sadistically persecutes his recruits in their early army training. (It is significant that the limits of military authority encountered in the book are set for the most part at N.C.O. level: once again there is the avoidance of wider issues such as class-friction—contrast *Erziehung vor Verdun*—or the efficiency of the command, a question raised as a matter of course in many of the British works.)

Acting as convenient foci for the resentment of Bäumer's generation, these two men are discussed and hated throughout the book, and their ultimate defeat is lingered over with affection. In the case of Himmelstoss, victory comes in three installments, culminating in the corporal's final humiliation on the field of battle, whereby a satisfying reversal of roles the boy-heroes are now the veterans and Himmelstoss the novice. The process of revenge takes us up to page 135, and only after the last drop of enjoyment has been wrung from the theme does the humiliation of the schoolmaster Kantorek take over to maintain this line of interest. He is reduced (like Professor Unrat) to a wreck, by the very methods applied by Himmelstoss against the boys themselves in basic training. But there are indications of the self-destructiveness of such a revenge-obsession for the adolescent mind. The child who apparently takes a delight in destroying the authority set over him is basically disturbed by his inability to put anything in its place. Here we touch on a theme central to Remarque's book and possibly central to the German experience of the destructiveness unleashed by the war: the vacuum that is left in the place of a discredited authority, and the unbearable responsibility for one's own future, cause a suffering as great as the physical horrors of war. If the lessons learnt at school do not apply at the front, it is equally true that the war has filled Remarque's soldiers with a knowledge that will alienate them totally from civilian life.

Appropriately, in view of the later course of German history, a sense of post-war purpose is conceived in no other terms but those of aggression against somebody or something. Most revealing of conditions in Germany in 1929 is the picture of resurrection after the war. The dead will march alongside the survivors to a new goal, but the vision collapses on the question, 'Marching? Against whom?'—'gegen wen?' The heroes' youthful antics can be seen as desperate attempts to assert individual freedom of action within a condition of total helplessness, which in turn could serve as a paradigm for the plight of the individual drawn along in the career-course of political developments in Weimar Germany.

In the war situation individuality is suspended; in *Im Westen* this point is made directly through the sheer size of military operations, demonstrated by terrible statistics and the masterly organization required to keep the war going. Indirectly, at the moment of death, loss of individuality is sketched in with reminders of particular human personalities, about to be obliterated forever. Remarque's warriors have a kind of typical individualism, as inalienable from them as a fingerprint and just as unremarkable. As annihilation threatens, one token characteristic serves as a reminder of the individuality which has been forfeited in war: 'Leer . . . verblutet rasch, niemand kann ihm helfen . . . Was nützt es ihm nun, daß er in der Schule ein so guter Mathematiker war.' Of another dying comrade, Kemmerich, it is said, 'Zigaretten konnte er nicht vertragen.' The situation which, rationally speaking, makes nonsense of individuality, in fact emphasizes the value of individual existence. (Hitler, too, was able to turn the helplessness of the 'armes Frontschwein' into a validation of existence.) Modern man, who *knows* his own individuality despite all the evidence of his reduction to collective anonymity, will be quick to take the point Remarque is making. In battle, the threat of death heightens the sense of individual life unbearably. Remarque injects a strong sensuality into the determination to survive, and much of the appeal of the novel is surely drawn from this vitality. There is an almost ecstatic feeling for the earth itself as the soldier under fire attempts to fuse himself with it. Again and again after the trenches the hunger for life is reborn. When the hero returns home on leave, his personal likes and dislikes suddenly become important again. The contrast with the impersonality of the front is too much for him, and he breaks down into a childish weakness. The war and his insignificance in the face of its vastness have literally been brought home to him.

Just as the sensation of threatened individuality is an experience common to the trenches and to life in Weimar Germany (though of course with a difference of acuteness), so the attempt at a solution, too, is shared. In *Im Westen*, *Kameradschaft* is raised to the level of a cult: and for many suffering from the dissensions, the lack of social cohesion, and the bewildering political diversity of Weimar, the comradeship of the war was indeed the object of a cult, especially for those at the extreme ends of the political spectrum. From the example of the moderate Remarque, however, it can be seen that extremes meet on this territory:

> Der Krieg hatte . . . die Erfahrung einer realen Gemeinschaft gebracht. Für einen großen Teil der Soldaten war diese 'Kameradschaft' Lebensbasis geworden. Im Nachkriegs-deutschland in dem wieder jeder auf sich gewiesen blieb, unter wirtschaftlich und politisch schwierigen Bedingungen, sehnten sich viele nach der Sicherheit der 'Kameradschaft' zurück, bauten sogar ihre Staatsvorstellung auf dem Verlangen nach ihr auf.

(This theme is taken up specifically in Remarque's own later novel *Der Weg zurück* (Berlin, 1931).) In *Im Westen* comradeship reaches an almost mystic intensity, to which is added a measure of adolescent hero-worship in

Bäumer's reverence for his older comrade and mentor, 'Kat.' (There is even a hint of latent adolescent homosexuality, for example in the disappointment in women experienced by the hero after his first sexual encounter, which implicitly serves merely to reinforce his love of his comrades; yet the disillusionment with females has an adolescent illogicality, too, since the women concerned are bought for the price of a loaf of bread, and their status as consumer objects is brought out by the pre-war advertising poster depicting a desirable young lady, which first whets the comrades' appetite for female company.)

Parallels to this *Kameradschaft*-cult are had to find in the British war-books. It is clear that in *Im Westen, Kameradschaft* bears the full weight of the soldiers' frustrated potential for idealism. Once again, the observation is as appropriate to Weimar as it is to Remarque's war.

Because of his characters' total immersion in war and lack of counterbalancing experience, Remarque clearly feels the need to supply certain safety valves to take off the pressure for his reader. Apart from the *Galgenhumor* of the troops, the main source of relief is the novel's overt sentimentality, as in the treatment of the hero's dying mother and the passage in which Bäumer describes himself as 'ein kleiner Soldat in der Frühe.' Before dismissing the latter as part of Remarque's bid for popular success, it would be apposite to remember that the novel conforms in this respect, as in so many others, to a characteristic tendency of *Neue Sachlichkeit*, described by Siegfried Kracauer in his influential book *Die Angestellten*: 'Nicht schlagender könnte sich das Geheimnis der neuen Sachlichkeit enthüllen . . . Nur einen Schritt in die Tiefe, und man weilt mitten in der üppigsten Sentimentalität.' Kracauer puts his finger on a 'popular' element which *Im Westen* possesses in good measure. But in the Weimar context sentimentality can be seen as a deliberate flouting of the pre-war aesthetic canon in the interests of democracy, related to the attack of *Neue Sachlichkeit* on authority in general.

Furthermore, in pragmatic terms, sentiment travels better than all but the best profundity. This brings us to the international, as against the internal, success of *Im Westen*. Partly it can be explained in rather crude terms: the novel represented the German soldier as a human being. In 1929 Germany was still an enigma to the outside world, and therefore an object of fear. By 1929 the British at least were beginning to try to understand their former enemies, to look for the common denominator and the definition of some area of agreement upon elementary and indisputable facts. The novel was increasingly regarded as a way of understanding the Germans, and by 1929 there was (in complete contrast to the pre-war dearth of translations) a score or so of German novelists whose work could be sampled in English.

None was as successful as Remarque in establishing the common denominator. One wonders, in fact, what part was played by this one book alone in creating that willingness to give the Germans one more chance to show that they were, after all, *human*, which ultimately led to Munich. Remarque may, in other words, have been influential in lulling his foreign readership into a false sense of security.

Remarque's novel possesses an unemphatic internationalism, largely by virtue of what it does *not* say. It sets up few barriers to acceptance in translation. This is not to say that it is in any sense an un-German book: it accurately reflects, as we have seen, German pride of arms as well as certain aspects of Weimar society. But, for example, no chauvinism is apparent in attitudes to the enemy. Indeed, no attitude is apparent except the practical kill-or-be-killed approach which survival dictates. The other side is simply 'die drüben': rarely is the nationality of the opposing troops identified. The shadowiness of the enemy contributes to the impersonality of Remarque's war, but at the same time it offers no hindrance to the willingness of a wide international readership to identify itself with Bäumer and his comrades. Even the aspects of trench life which are specifically German will tend to increase the sympathy of the foreign reader, rather than stand in its way. The German soldier was far worse fed and worse supplied than his Allied counterpart. At one point we are told that the corned beef and butter and white bread to be captured in the Allied trenches are now the major reason for pressing forward to the attack, and no one will fail to understand a half-starved man in the front line who attacks to eat. Even the claim put forward by Remarque's narrator that Germany was not defeated, but simply overwhelmed by the Allies' wealth of men and materiel, need not have the effect of alienating the non-German reader, since it is a fair statement of well-known facts, and a corrective to the dangerous contemporary propaganda, the so-called *Dolchstoßlegende*, which holds that Germany could have won but for the treachery of her politicians.

In the lack of differentiation of attitudes to enemy soldiers we strike against one of the limits of Remarque's documentation. Discussion of such matters certainly took place in all armies and is a commonplace in most other war-books. But whatever the reason for the failure to record some aspects of the war, the result is to increase the universality of the book's appeal. The analysis of German civilian society is equally undelineated (apart from Remarque's obvious hatred of the medical profession). The nature of Weimar society (artistic and cultural life apart) being essentially conservative, Remarque's German leaders would not in any case have thanked him for an analysis which specifically demanded changes in their own social arrangements. His social criticism is confined almost entirely to exceptional wartime conditions and lacks any kind of *Appellcharakter*, or demand for action. There is the familiar lack of comprehension of the civilian for the front-line soldier, to be found in the majority of First World War books. There is the hatred of *Etappenschweine* and non-combatant soldiers. There is the sentiment, heartily endorsed in other war-books by veterans of both sides, that 'the wrong people are fighting here.' There is bitter criticism of the people sitting safely at home talking of the need for a breakthrough. Equally familiar, and even more bitter, there is criticism of the industrialists growing fat on the profits of the war. The title of the novel itself, strikingly echoed in Aldington's *Death of a Hero*, is equally international, encapsulating as it does the soldiers' awareness of the loss of interest among those at home as the war settles down into an 'uneventful' stalemate ('all quiet on the Western Front' is the familiar newspaper report of the later war years). Tacitly it suggests the solidarity of the fighting man in all armies against his real enemy, the civilian authority and civilian society—including the soldier's own family—in so far as it supports authority; which, in general, it blindly does. (See the 'Nutwood Manor' section of Sassoon's *Memoirs of an Infantry Officer* for an example of the complete gulf between the front-line soldier and the society of which he was formerly a complaisant member.)

Towards the end of *Im Westen* the moral collapse of authority becomes so obvious to the soldier—and here the German experience is closer to the French than to the British —that there is vague talk of making an end to the war and of revolution of an unspecified nature. This belongs mainly to the experience of the losing side, of course. It is a feature which, like Remarque's pacifism, can have done little to disturb the equilibrium of the average bourgeois reader. It is an illogicality, but a very human one, that even if we concede that war is meaningless at any time, it appears infinitely less meaningful when defeat becomes inevitable. Though in rational terms pacifism is more convincing in the victor, it is emotionally more acceptable in the defeated.

Im Westen nichts Neues comes close to being all things to all men. It is a pacifist novel, yet it could be seen and has been seen as a glorification of the German soldier and of the war. The war was distant enough in 1929 to be discussed and thought about again; and yet it was not decent for it to be depicted without reservation as heroic and exemplary. One can imagine that the pacifist framework of *Im Westen* salved the conscience of the crypto-militarist or the prurient reader reliving the horrors of 1914–18. Looking at the book in a different perspective, however, we see that through its democratic interest in the small man whom the war devours, the novel says a good deal about Germany in the late twenties. Indeed, since the society of Weimar Germany, of which it was a product, was a forcing-ground for many developments of twentieth-century European society, the very indebtedness of the book to its origins may have helped to make it something of a monument, and contributed to its lasting reputation.

CHRISTINE R. BARKER AND R. W. LAST

The Critics' Views of All Quiet on the Western Front

In 1936, the National Socialist newspaper *Völkischer Beobachter* made this proud announcement to its readers:

> After all the lies told by people like Remarque, we now bring to you the experience of a soldier who took part in the war, of which you will say at once: that is what it was really like.

There then follows an extract from an account of life at the front which, on closer examination, turns out to be nothing other than part of Remarque's *Im Westen nichts Neues* (presumably sent in anonymously by a third party), and this really was heaping insult on injury, since Joseph Goebbels's *Angriff* had already been similarly duped into printing a "genuine tale from the front line" at the height of his anti-Remarque campaign, which had also turned out to have been culled from the pages of *Im Westen nichts Neues*. These were among the more bizarre consequences of the publication of what rapidly became one of the most successful books ever written—that is, if success is to be measured in terms of the number of copies sold, a proposition which many might be inclined to challenge.

When *Im Westen nichts Neues* was serialized in the *Vossische Zeitung* in November and December 1928, the paper's circulation tripled as eager

---

From *Erich Maria Remarque*. © 1979 Oswald Wolff Publishers Ltd. (Original title: *All Quiet on the Western Front*.)

readers snatched the latest issue from the news vendors with an avidity matched only by those in quest of the latest news of Pickwick or the fate of Little Nell in nineteenth-century England. The book edition, preceded by a concentrated advertising campaign in the press and on street hoardings, sold a million copies in a single year; its author was nominated for the Nobel literature prize; and the work set in train the most amazing storm of controversy, in the course of which it was hailed by one faction as the greatest anti-war novel of all time, denounced by the National Socialists as denigratory to the German *Volk*, and ultimately burned in the Opernplatz in Berlin during the infamous Nazi book-burning ceremony on 10 May 1933 (in such distinguished company as the works of Thomas and Heinrich Mann, Kästner, Brecht, Joyce, Hemingway and Gorki), to the accompaniment of these solemn words:

> As a protest against the literary betrayal of the soldiers of the Great War, and on behalf of the education of our people in the spirit of truth, I consign to the flames the writings of Erich Maria Remarque.

Remarque found himself pilloried by his opponents, and accused of all manner of misrepresentation and misconduct; books and articles galore were written about him and his bestseller, many of them factually inaccurate, not to say libellous; a parody appeared, transposing the setting from the Western front to the Greek camp outside the walls of Troy; and the writer and critic Dr Salomo Friedlaender, under his pseudonym of Mynona, published a full-length attack on Remarque and his masterpiece in mediocrity, as he was pleased to call it.

Not surprisingly, the circumstances surrounding the composition of *Im Westen nichts Neues* and its submission to publishing houses are surrounded with confusion and contradictions. One thing, however, is clear, and that is that Remarque did not compose the novel as a deliberate money-making exercise, as Rowley for one seems to indicate: "The particular blend of suffering, sensuality and sentiment suggests that Remarque had gauged public taste." In an interview with Axel Eggebrecht in 1929, Remarque presents his own reasons for writing the novel. He had, he states, been suffering from serious bouts of depression, the underlying cause of which remained a mystery to him until he made a sustained effort to ascertain why his mood was so consistently bleak:

> It was through these deliberate acts of self-analysis that I found my way back to my war experiences. I could observe a similar

phenomenon in many of my friends and acquaintances. The shadow of war hung over us, especially when we tried to shut our minds to it. The very day this thought struck me, I put pen to paper, without much in the way of prior thought.

Working quickly during the evenings after doing a day's work at the offices of *Sport im Bild*, Remarque completed the novel in a mere six weeks—keeping himself awake with strong cigars and large quantities of coffee, if we are to believe a rather inflated account by Riess, who also cuts the time of composition in half.

The finished work was submitted to S. Fischer Verlag, the celebrated publishers of that other great German success of this century, Thomas Mann's *Buddenbrooks*, who were an obvious choice for any novelist eager to establish a solid reputation for himself. The manuscript was read by Bermann Fischer, who is recorded as having said that, to the best of his recollection,

> he read the novel at a single sitting, the night before a month's holiday touring, placed it before Samuel Fischer on the following morning and urged him to read it at once and draw up a contract with the author without delay, before any other publishers got sight of it.

Bermann Fischer was convinced that he had brought off a really outstanding coup, but Samuel Fischer would go no further than to tell Remarque that he would take the book if no other publisher was prepared to accept it. When he heard about this, Bermann Fischer anxiously sought to retrieve the manuscript from Remarque, but by this time it was too late.

Remarque records that Samuel Fischer had informed him that, in his opinion, the book would not sell, since no one wanted to hear about the war anymore. But the real reason was that Samuel Fischer had very fixed ideas about what his firm should or should not put into print, and he was convinced that *Im Westen nichts Neues* did not accord with his notion of a work suitable for publication under the Fischer imprint, and he held to this view, apparently without a trace of regret, even when the novel turned out to be a huge and instantaneous success.

In the Eggebrecht interview, Remarque does not refer to the Fischer episode, but this seems more attributable to the fact that he was a reluctant interviewee than to any more sinister motive on his part; instead, he simply states that the manuscript lay untouched in his writing desk for close on six months until, at the insistence of friends, he put it in the hands of Ullstein's Propyläen Verlag.

As to the exact circumstances of its acceptance by Ullstein, there was a brief, if acrimonious, exchange of views in the correspondence columns of the *Frankfurter Allgemeine Zeitung* in 1962. Professor Paul Frischauer claimed that it was he who came to know Remarque when the latter was working for *Sport im Bild*, and as a result of their meeting mentioned *Im Westen nichts Neues* to Dr Franz Ullstein at a social gathering. Ullstein then ensured that the work was seen by his reader Max Krell, who instantly recognized its qualities. So much for Professor Frischauer's account; Ullstein himself went on record as stating that it was a certain Herr Ross who first read it and strongly recommended its acceptance. In his memoirs, Krell does at least confirm that the novel came on to his desk shortly after Whitsun 1928.

Whatever the details, the Propyläen Verlag decided to give the work the full treatment: it was to come out first in instalments in the *Vossische Zeitung* and then—in a slightly revised form—in a blaze of publicity in a first edition of 50,000 copies. The rest is history.

The reaction to the novel in Germany was violent in the extreme, and opinions soon polarized; but it is instructive to turn first to the response on the other side of the Channel, where a more stable political climate and the fact that Britain was not smarting under a humiliating defeat and the crippling terms of the Versailles treaty enabled the novel to be considered more dispassionately, first and foremost as a piece of literature rather than as a political manifesto.

The traditionally anonymous reviewer in the *Times Literary Supplement* accorded *Im Westen nichts Neues* a muted reception when it appeared in English translation by A. W. Wheen under the title *All Quiet on the Western Front*, published by Putnam for the princely sum of seven shillings and sixpence. The reviewer expresses surprise at the outstanding popularity of the work, which sold, as he records, 275,000 copies in just over six weeks:

> Very good as it undoubtedly is, this figure is astonishing; and one finds oneself wondering whether an extra nought has not slipped in.

The *Times Literary Supplement* article sets the pattern for other English reviews, both in the slight note of incredulity at such success attending a novel of this nature and also in the careful reading which the reviewer undertakes of the work on its own merits which, even at this early stage, resulted in the emergence of interesting if somewhat inaccurate observations, such as the suggestion that the tale is "obviously autobiographical," or that "the real hero of the story is the narrator's particular friend, Katczinsky."

Im Westen nichts Neues in its English guise must have come as a welcome change from the tidal wave of what might be dubbed the "soft porn" of war literature flooding the British market. On the column adjacent to the *Times Literary Supplement* review, an advertiser announces—with unwitting irony and uncomfortable propinquity—the publication of *War Birds*:

> Still the best-selling war book. Life, death, praying, cursing, women and the snarl of shrapnel! All the wild ecstasy and stark tragedy in this unexpurgated diary of a flying man!

The advertisement closes with a glowing extract from the review of *War Birds* by Gerald Gould of the *Daily Express*, who must have been busily preparing to eat his words: "It is the finest book on the war that has ever appeared, and a finer will never be written!"

The *Times Literary Supplement* reviewer also takes up one issue raised in the lurid apotheosis of *War Birds*, namely, that the novel contains references to certain areas of life not normally discussed in polite company and, significantly, he adds that such references are "of a type that (the reader) will not find in English novels." This prudish British insularity was particularly strong in the 1920's; indeed, it had continued unabated from the early years of the century, and is epitomized by the chauvinistic assertion in Erskine Childer's anti-German spy novel, *The Riddle of the Sands*: "It was something in his looks and manner, you know how different we are from foreigners."

The review in *The New Statesman* reflects a similar cast of mind, and points out in mitigation that, of course, the Germans had the worst of it in the Great War,

> for on that side everything was a little more so—militarism was a little more militaristic; parade ground imbecilities were a little more imbecile; the squalor of the trenches (in the last year or two) was more squalid.

And it concludes on a not untypical note of faint praise, commending the strengths of the work on the one hand, yet on the other stating that this level of achievement was not beyond the reach of any competent writer who happened to have served in the trenches:

> For the rest, anyone who was sufficiently in the thick of it for a long period, on one side or the other, might have written this grim, monotonous record, if he had the gift, which the author

has, of remembering clearly, and setting down his memories truly, in naked and violent words.

Grudging though the recognition may have been in many quarters, the reception of *Im Westen nichts Neues* in Britain did at least focus attention on the novel as literature, but, when we turn to the reaction within Remarque's home country, it is clear that we find ourselves faced with an entirely different situation.

In Germany, the emphasis was not so much on the book as on the impact which it had on individuals and political factions alike. All the varied reactions have one thing in common, as can be illustrated by the case of the angry Doctor of Medicine Karl Kroner, writing in the *Neue Preussische Kreuz-Zeitung*, who protests mendaciously that nowhere in *Im Westen nichts Neues* is the medical profession depicted with humanity or sympathy. Even the ancillary staff, he complains, come off badly. No one would believe from Remarque's novel that there were actually doctors up in the front line itself, facing the same dangers as the troops in action. Remarque, claims Dr Kroner, gives the totally erroneous impression that the wounded soldier was obliged to pick his own way back to the field stations. And, worse still,

> all the old tales of horror about the Germans, now happily long forgotten, and which sprang up in the war psychosis, will now be resurrected. People abroad will draw the following conclusions: if German doctors deal with their own fellow countrymen in this manner, what acts of inhumanity will they not perpetrate against helpless prisoners delivered up into their hands or against the populations of occupied territory?

Dr Kroner reads *Im Westen nichts Neues* as documentary fiction, as if it staked some kind of claim to being representative both of German attitudes and German actions at the front and behind the lines during the Great War.

The novel is also regarded as aspiring to present the "truth" on a literal, autobiographical level. The *Times Literary Supplement* and *New Statesmen* reviewers were far from being alone in their insistence that the reader is being presented with an account of events that actually took place, and more than one critic has gone so far as to chastise Remarque for not giving precise details of time or place, so that they might be checked for accuracy. A certain Peter Kropp, who had been a patient in the same military hospital at Duisberg as Remarque, and who knew him, as Erich Remark, of course, was outraged at his former comrade's descriptions of the hospital in *Im Westen nichts Neues*. Remarque, he protests, presents a very partial view which is not without its serious inaccuracies. Of course there was a great deal of suffering in the hospital, but there was much silent heroism too. The hospital, asserts Kropp, was run in an exemplary fashion, the patients were tended by a nursing order of Catholic nuns, and Remarque is entirely erroneous in his assertion that the patients were disturbed by the noisy praying of the sisters in the corridors. Kropp goes on to describe the exact location of the chapel in the hospital, thus "proving" that their prayers could not have been heard by the wounded soldiers, as Remarque claims in his novel. From this point, Kropp proceeds to try and identify individual patients with characters in the novel, and lights in particular on the forty-year-old Lewandowski, who has been in the hospital for ten months, and who in the novel is excitedly anticipating a first visit from his wife. Lewandowski tells the others—"for in the army we have no secrets of that kind"—that he is desperate to make love to his wife when she comes to see him, and the others stand guard as the blushing couple embrace in the hospital bed. This is too much for Kropp, who protests that this kind of thing simply could not have happened: "I should certainly have known about it," he complains.

In more general terms, Kropp castigates Remarque for accentuating the negative:

> I find no front-line spirit in Remark's book. There were other front-line soldiers who were different from the way Remark depicts them. There were such soldiers to whom the protection of homeland, protection of house and homestead, protection of the family was their highest objective, and to whom this will to protect their homeland gave the strength to endure any extremities.

This assumption that, in *Im Westen nichts Neues*, Remarque was seeking to encapsulate a piece of personal and national history in literary form was immediately taken up by both sides in the critical debate.

In his celebrated review for *Die literarische Welt*, the dramatist Ernst Toller claims that Remarque "has spoken on behalf of all of us." Not only does the book describe in unforgettably graphic terms the horrific experiences and privations to which the front-line soldier was exposed, but so exemplary is it, Toller argues, that it should be read by everyone as an anti-war document, and especially in the schools. *Im Westen nichts Neues* says more about the nation and its involvement in the Great War than any statistics or weighty historical tomes ever could.

A publicity pamphlet produced by the Ullstein Propyläen Verlag entitled *Der Kampf um Remarque* (The Battle over Remarque), which consists of a compilation of criticism, both positive and negative, of *Im Westen nichts Neues*, cites a letter from a war-blinded schoolteacher who welcomes the novel with open arms as the one book with which to instruct the minds of the young on the subject of the Great War. This work, he writes, fortuitously employing a turn of phrase which, as we shall see later, is crucial to a proper understanding of the novel, represents "my own release (=Erlösung) from the front."

Almost alone among the reviews of *Im Westen nichts Neues*, the Berlin *Die Welt am Montag*, quoted in the Propyläen Verlag pamphlet, at least begins to spell out the nature of the real problem posed by the novel:

> What makes it so unique? . . . the fact that Remarque does not spoon-feed his reader page by page with ready-made attitudes, but leaves him to draw his own conclusions from the book.

But, by and large, *Im Westen nichts Neues* came to be regarded by the vast majority of people as the anti-war book *par excellence* (or the worst kind of pacifist propaganda, depending on which camp one belonged to), a successor to Bertha von Suttner's *Die Waffen nieder!* (Lay down your Arms, 1892), which had been instrumental in giving an early impetus to the International Arbitration and Peace Association because of its stark portrayal of the horrors of war, not least in its famous depiction of the heroine, Martha von Tilling, picking her way among the dead and dying on the battlefield of Königgrätz in search of her missing husband. Suttner it was who persuaded her life-long admirer, the industrialist Alfred Nobel, to institute his peace prize, one of whose recipients she became in 1905. But, although this peace movement outlived the First World War in various forms, it had already passed its second peak in Germany before the appearance of *Im Westen nichts Neues*, and the right-wing backlash was already in full swing; and, as Shuster has pointed out, "the excesses of the earlier pacifism only served to swell the forces which were now ushering in a rebirth of militarism."

This militarism assumed two forms in the context of the onslaught launched against *Im Westen nichts Neues* and its author. In its milder manifestation, it outraged all those who were instinctively appalled at the desecration, as they saw it, both of the sacrifices made by the front-line soldiers and of the idea of the German nation. The most closely-argued contemporary critical attack on the novel by Heisler states that, for all its undoubted merits, the work represents a threat, since it tends to sap the energies of the German nation at a time when it has to assert itself in the face of a hostile world if it is to survive.

Not unexpectedly, the main opposition to *Im Westen nichts Neues* came from the National Socialists, who regarded the book—which, as they were not slow to point out, was produced by a Jewish publisher—as part of a well-financed international conspiracy on the part of Bolshevists and Jews against the German *Volk*. At that time, the theorists of National Socialism were claiming insistently that the Great War represented nothing less than the fire in which the spirit of the emergent German Reich had been forged, and that, as a consequence, *Im Westen nichts Neues* constituted a betrayal of all that is great and noble in Germany and the German nation.

Remarque is accused of partiality in his depiction of the front-line soldier, since he presents only "how a few emotionally unbalanced people conducted themselves before they ever went into battle." What the National Socialists found most offensive in Remarque's portrayal of the men in the trenches was his demythologizing of front-line warfare, of the concept of the "hero" which is so crucial to the National Socialist foundation myth. Life, it is argued, is a relentless Darwinian struggle, in which the individual, if he is to survive, has to assert himself in the face of others; and similarly, the strongest nation is the one that has the will to survive more successfully than any of its rivals. The individual cannot exist as a separate selfish entity—to coin a phrase, no man is an island—since he is part of a greater whole, the race or nation, and the selfless surrender of his own life on the part of the hero in order that the whole might survive, is the greatest and noblest act that a human being can perform.

Remarque's negative attitude to war in general was equally anathema to the National Socialists in that it embodied two of their *bêtes noires*: namely, pacifism and internationalism. The proponents of internationalism may proclaim from the rooftops that the life of the individual is the highest good, but the ineluctable laws of nature, which antedate the appearance of man on this planet and to which he is subordinate, dictate that this simply is not so. In a grotesque prefiguration of the biogeneticists' concept of "non-selfish" behaviour, the National Socialists argue that it is the survival of the race, the nation, that matters, not that of the individual. Hence internationalism which is more or less equated with Marxism, is, like pacifism, a dangerous aberration: "Pacifism is the same heresy on the ethical plane as is Marxism in the social sphere." If the life of the individual is sacred, as the pacifists claim, then how much more sacred must be the life of the nation:

> The projected utopia of the pacifists has one thing in common with that of the Marxists—and that is, that it will never be realized. As long as men are men, as long as death remains a fact of life, its twin servants, sickness and war, will remain with us too.

Disease is equated with war, and the argument goes that getting rid of doctors will not result in the disappearance of disease, but will inevitably bring about its spread and ultimate domination. Therefore the soldier is not fomenting war and militarism; on the contrary, he is actually fighting *against* war, just like the doctor combatting disease.

This insidiously plausible line of argumentation was brought to bear with particular force on the figures in *Im Westen nichts Neues* who violated the notion of the Great War as a positive rather than a destructive force—regrettable though it was, of course, and rendered necessary only by the aggression of others:

> The war was a test; in the thunder of the cannon all masks fell away, and men stood there naked, in their true qualities. He who had eyes to see and ears to hear learned at the front to distinguish the wheat from the chaff.

And, in contrast to Remarque's negative concept of comradeship, the community of soldiers at the front in reality paved the way for the new national community of the coming Reich, under the leadership of the Führer, of course.

Despite their vocal protest, the National Socialists were unable to prevent the publication and sale of *Im Westen nichts Neues*, but Joseph Goebbels, at the time Gauleiter of the Berlin section of the National Socialist party, found himself presented with a golden opportunity to bring off a major propaganda coup when the celebrated American film based on the book, *All Quiet on the Western Front*, was screened in the German capital. The film, directed by Lewis Milestone and produced by Universal Pictures, was one of the early talkies and has since come to be recognized as one of the great classics of the cinema. The National Socialists seemed to be losing the initiative in the parliamentary battle in the *Reichstag*, but Goebbels leaped at this unique chance of bringing the fight out on to the streets. He organized a gang of Hitler Youth to storm the auditorium where the film was to be premiered, and they rampaged through the building, hurling stink bombs, scattering white mice and shouting "Germany awake!" Goebbels's tactic of stirring up controversy over an issue at the centre of public attention certainly paid off; not only did he attract considerable publicity, he even succeeded in getting the film banned in Germany. And, as we saw earlier, the book itself was also burned—and banned—when the dream of a Third Reich became a political reality in 1933.

Remarque was also the object of attack from a quite different quarter, this time on largely unpolitical grounds. The slight but acid parody *Vor Troja nichts Neues* (All Quiet before the Walls of Troy), supposedly by one Emil Marius Requark, has an overweening first-person narrator whose sole ambition it is to amass great wealth after the war is over: "I will become a rich man, all Greece will read my book." And, in fact, the whole Trojan war seems to be taking place simply so that he can write a book about it. Nor is the narrator inclined to underestimate his own abilities: "One has such incredibly clever thoughts and one gets to feel the importance of one's person." He inflates his ego to its fullest extent and proclaims: "Thus it is that I am writing a war diary. It will contain a great deal about me and just a very little about the war." The rest of the world is in a state of utter confusion; the soldiers alone have retained their clear-sightedness and integrity.

The great poet Homer is also present, compiling the official version of the war and evidently enjoying himself. The narrator, hearing him mutter hexameters out loud, assumes that he is inebriated, and bids him forget about noble heroes and all that kind of thing and write instead about the sordid realties of war, the mud and the lice (to which latter the narrator has, it seems, become quite attached). The soldiers, as a sentence picked out in large type stresses, "belong to a generation which will never recover from the impact of war. Our lives are ruined beyond recall." The parody in *Vor Troja nichts Neues* is directed partly against Remarque's pacifist tendencies, but even more against his personal vanity in arrogating to himself the rôle of the omniscient recording angel of the Great War, the sole repository of the whole truth abut the armed conflict on the Western front.

This latter view is also espoused by Mynona's *Hat Erich Maria Remarque wirklich gelebt?* an exceedingly witty and entirely libelous assault on Remarque, which follows the pattern of Mynona's equally venomous onslaught on Freud, in the publisher's announcement for which he is elevated to the dubious status of the "Chaplin of German philosophy." Employing the time-honoured principle that the least strenuous means of demolishing the work is to discredit the man, Mynona summons up every pun, turn of wit, and allusion to his victim's life, employment and previous writing—especially his advertising career (there is much play on Conti-dummies for babies and the like) and, of course, *Die Traumbude*—in his character assassination attempt, and tops the whole thing off with a "Documentary Appendix for Sceptics" quoting Remarque's birth certificate and other information "proving" that he falsely assumed the French tail on his name. The book closes with a list of "Erich Maria Remark's Collected Werques" (sic). He finds Remarque guilty of outstanding mediocrity, and expresses his utter astonishment that such a thoroughly ordinary piece of pen-pushing should have attracted such a hugely disproportionate amount of public attention and stand at the epicentre of such an earth-shattering storm of controversy.

Osnabrück—"the mouse that gave birth to this mountain"—has a great deal to answer for, claims Mynona, since in *Im Westen nichts Neues* that town's celebrated son does little more than hold up a dull mirror to a drab age. Mynona reminds his readers of the orator in Classical times who started with fright when he received universal applause, fearful that he might have said something ridiculous, for "only the uttermost folly gains instant thunderous approbation, the truth in contrast is greeted by an audience of deaf mutes."

Mynona describes his attack as a satirical apotheosis; but, in reality, it is no more than an enormous ego-trip, a romp of *Schadenfreude* on the part of a writer who really ought to have known better. His attack becomes more understandable—but even less forgivable—when it is realized that, under his real appellation of Dr Salomo Friedlaender, Mynona was a less than successful poet and writer, a minor member of the circle of contributors to the Expressionist periodical *Der Sturm* with pretensions as a philosopher in the wake of Nietzsche. He had, he was convinced, "solved" the post-Kantian dilemma of subjectivity and the destruction of absolute values by means of a strong creative individual operating a positive, but still subjective ethic. Unfortunately, no one was inclined to listen to him. And nothing could have been more repugnant to the aspirations of Dr Friedlaender than the attitudes of the characters in *Im Westen nichts Neues*. The instinctive revulsion on the part of Mynona, of our anonymous parodist, and indeed of others, to the popularity of this work prefigures most of what little critical attention the novel has been accorded in the West in recent years.

Im Westen nichts Neues hardly receives more than a passing—and not always accurate—mention in histories of contemporary literature published in the West: Soergel and Hohoff only accord it a handful of lines in a nine-page section on the First World War in literature, stating that "in the case of Remarque, too, comradeship and sacrifice were values which outlived the war" (the first part of the assertion may be true, the second certainly is not); a five-hundred page compendium on German literature in the Weimar Republic is even more parsimonious, squeezing out just three mentions of *Im Westen nichts Neues* by title in a whole section devoted exclusively to the novel of the Great War; Lange, skating across the surface of modern literature between 1870 and 1940, simply refers to the novel as "one of the first, but not one of the most substantial of the war books," an *ex cathedra* pronouncement not untypical of this brand of general survey; a more considered reaction from Rühle none the less insists that the work is political and pacifist, which "explains the hypnotic mass impact of the novel and its effectiveness as a pacifist manifesto"; and Kerker goes to the other extreme in a somewhat idiosyncratic interpretation of the work, in which he claims that, far from being an anti-war novel, it actually helped to bring about the Second World War, but he is clearly confusing analysis of the novel as such with the impact which it happened to have in certain quarters.

Of the handful of scholars who have undertaken detailed consideration of *Im Westen nichts Neues* in the West, Liedloff has some kind words to say about it, but his attention is diverted by the fact that he is writing a descriptive comparatist essay, relating it to Hemingway's *A Farewell to Arms*; Swados defends the artistic value of the novel, praising its directness in depicting the horrors of war; in another comparatist study, this time with reference to F. Manning's *Her Privates We*, Klein underlines the literary merit of *Im Westen nichts Neues* and stresses its highly organized structure, although he does not go into a great deal of detail on this vital issue; and Rowley, in a sensitive essay, echoes Klein's views about the novel's structure, and stresses that the style—which he dubs "journalistic"—is deliberately chosen by Remarque, and not a sign of weakness on his part.

One suspects that the scant attention now paid to Remarque in the West is attributable, in part at least, to the huge success of the work—for how, the argument goes in the groves of academe, can something so overwhelmingly popular be great literature in an age when the true artist seems inevitably to be alienated from the public at large? Such considerations seem to loom particularly large for the German academic critic: witness, for example, the very mixed reception accorded to a dramatist like Fritz Hochwälder, who insists on writing "well-made plays" when everyone knows they are *passé* in an era of theatrical experimentation, or another dramatist, Rolf Hochhuth, who actually has the nerve to write about individual responsibility when the fashionable critic has long since pronounced it dead and buried—both, needless to say, very successful writers who have attracted a large public following. And, apart from the issue as to whether the novel can be regarded as "serious literature" or not, *Im Westen nichts Neues* has become almost totally submerged under the weight of the political and ideological battles that have been waged around it.

In the East, on the other hand, there have been no aesthetic reservations, for the social—not to say socialist—content of a work far outweighs any such decadent Western consideration, and *Im Westen nichts Neues* has attracted a fair amount of interest in academic circles there, largely as an illustration of a liberal Western piece which, on the social plane, puts a finger on the evils of the world but regrettably goes no further.

With not untypical circular argumentation, Marxist critics assert that the novel *is* political despite itself—its inability to advocate positive action being itself regarded as the assumption of a political stand. The principal complaint of the Marxist critic is that *Im Westen nichts Neues* fails in its social obligations: having recognized the disease, it avoids taking the next logical step, that of pronouncing a means (Marxist-Leninist, perhaps?) towards a cure. Remarque, and others like him, "indeed recognized the growing Fascist threat but did not have the will to make the revolutionary response to it."

So the wheel turns full circle, and once more *Im Westen nichts Neues* is regarded as a representative work, but this time it is criticized for failing to draw any positive conclusions from the evils it detects and depicts in the militarism of Germany in World War One, which at least makes a change from being attacked for not being militaristic enough.

The novel is also found wanting on the grounds that, in its portrayal of the war scene, it is too limited in perspective: in presenting, for example, the martinet figure of the corporal Himmelstoss, Remarque is accused of concentrating shortsightedly on the symptoms, not the root cause, and for this reason if for no other the novel is incapable of advancing any kind of positive solution. Left-wing totalitarianism comes close to its arch-enemy, Fascism, when one Marxist critic, Wegner, complains that Remarque is only depicting the "little man" of the time who needs, but lacks entirely, some sense of spiritual direction, a purposeful rôle for himself in society. One can almost hear a demand for the *Führerprinzip* behind these words.

Hardly any of the host of reviewers, critics and political theorists who have put pen to paper on the subject of *Im Westen nichts Neues*—or, more frequently, on issues raised by the novel—have made any real contribution to a proper understanding of the actual work itself; in fact, most of them have succeeded in going beyond the point at which the novel ceases to be relevant to their discussion. The first English critics tended to misconstrue it because of its "foreign-ness"; the Germans because it was used as ammunition in the battle between the liberals and pacifists on the one hand and the militarists and National Socialists on the other; and, after the Second World War, Western critics were either preoccupied with whether or not it was fit to be considered as "art" at all, or were again busily looking at the circumstances surrounding the work, either as comparatists or practitioners of the currently fashionable art of the aesthetics of the reception of literature; and, behind the Iron Curtain, the Marxist critics have been holding it up against the yardstick of social and political commitment and finding it wanting.

But, for all that, *Im Westen nichts Neues*—like many another work—has managed to survive its critics; yet the main issue still remains largely unanswered: What makes it such a compelling and successful work? And the only way to answer that question is actually to take a look at the novel itself.

Im Westen nichts Neues concerns the war experiences of a school class of young men who volunteer for active service under patriotic pressure from Kantorek, their schoolmaster, and another group of men whom they have closely befriended in the army. Of the class, originally twenty in all, only a handful remain, and the attention is focused on four of them—Kropp, Müller, Leer and Bäumer—and this quartet is balanced by four others: Tjaden, a mechanic, Westhus, a turf-cutter, Detering, a farmer, and Katczinsky (referred to by the nickname of "Kat"), at forty the oldest of the group.

This numerical equilibrium which Remarque establishes between the more intelligent but inexperienced young soldiers on the one hand and the academically less able ex-workers on the other, who compensate for their lack of intellectual attainment by a wider experience of life, points to a strong sense of organization on the part of the author which, as we shall see in due course, is fundamental to the entire work and has been studiously ignored by most critics.

It is told, principally in the historic present (which will be retained in quotations although it rings awkwardly in English), by a first-person narrator, Paul Bäumer, whose surname has been assiduously dismembered by Liedloff into "Baum" (= tree) and "Träumer" (dreamer), which by a tangential leap of the imagination is caused to represent two supposedly key constituents of Bäumer's nature: his "yearning for beauty" encapsulated in the "organic growth" of the tree; and his reflective and inward-turned personality. However, there is not a shred of evidence, internal or external, which might indicate that this is anything other than a perfectly ordinary German name, chosen precisely because of its ordinariness. The "Paul," on the other hand, is a direct reference to Remarque's original second Christian name and suggests that the novel is obliquely autobiographical. (Until Mynona dredged up the "truth" about Remarque's "real" name, of course, that autobiographical element remained hidden from the reader.) The problem is, to what extent and in what manner does it reflect the life and convictions of the author? This question could equally be posed in relation to the vast majority of Remarque's output. Critics—especially those hostile towards *Im Westen nichts Neues*—have all too eagerly tended to fall into the trap of arguing themselves into a logically absurd position: on the one hand, Remarque is castigated for not adhering faithfully to the "facts" of his own personal life, and yet on the other he is reprimanded by the same people for presenting a personal, partial and biased picture of the war on the Western front.

To some extent, at least, Remarque is to blame for this state of affairs; he describes the experiences and emotions of his central figure with such vividness and with such an aura of authenticity that one is all too readily tempted to assume that the events described actually took place precisely as he depicts them, or, if they did not, that some kind of fraud is being perpetrated; it is, to borrow an observation from an entirely different context, "a reproof to that large body of readers, who, when a novelist has really carried conviction to them, assert off-hand: 'O, that must be autobiography!'" The sentiments are Remarque's, the words those of Arnold Bennett.

The most superficial examination of, say, place-names, in *Im Westen nichts Neues*, makes it abundantly clear that Remarque has selectively plundered his own past experiences and environment in the composition of his novel. When Bäumer (why do critics patronizingly tend to refer to him as "Paul" all the time?) is entering his home town by train on leave from the front, for example, he passes over the Bremer Strasse before entering the main station. And there is no denying that the railway line to Remarque's home town of Osnabrück does precisely that (but the more pernickety critic might have observed that this is the route from the *east*, and therefore less likely to have been travelled upon by a soldier returning from the Western front). When Bäumer leaves the station, he sees the river rushing out from the sluices under the mill bridge; he looks up at the old watch tower, now used as a wash house; he crosses the bridge, finds his way home, climbs the stairs to his parents' flat, and later sits at his bedroom window looking out at the chestnut tree in the garden of the inn across the way—and every detail is "almost photographically accurate."

Although Remarque keeps close to reality in his depiction of the setting of his home town, leaving the front line deliberately imprecise because of its uniformity of appearance and the irrelevance of geographical designations, there is much less to be found in the way of parallels between the characters and their actions and any real life equivalents, save on the most superficial level: Bäumer's class "volunteers" under the chiding tongue of Kantorek, whereas all but three of Remarque's class waited until they were conscripted in 1916 (including our author himself). Other parallels are more or less on the level of, for example, the name of the corporal Himmelstoss being based on that of a family living in the Jahnstrasse in Osnabrück.

So it is quite evident that we are considering here a writer who, by preference, draws fairly directly but none the less selectively on his own experiences and background, although he is by no means seeking to present us with fictionalized autobiography. The reader unfamiliar with the topography of Osnabrück is not one whit the poorer. Were it not for all the nonsense penned about Remarque and his supposed "distortions" of reality, it would hardly be necessary to state the obvious; namely, that Remarque uses his home town or city and experiences close to his own as a convenient basis for his imaginative work.

Instead of fussing about the supposed authenticity or otherwise of Remarque's work, it might be less quixotic to consider the internal parallels between novel and reality. In order to do so, we must return to the words of the blind schoolteacher in the Propyläen publicity pamphlet, for whom the novel represented a release or "Erlösung" from the experiences of the war, a cathartic purging of the emotional residue of the front line. It enabled him to sort out within himself the tangled memories and emotions of the Great War, and to come to terms with them. And it is precisely in this light that Remarque himself regarded *Im Westen nichts Neues*. In the interview with Eggebrecht, Remarque too talks of a sense of release that came with the writing of his novel, and he uses exactly the same word, "Erlösung." He had experienced an inexplicable sense of depression, and the act of writing had enabled him to recognize the symptoms and their cause and to work towards some kind of accommodation with the past.

But more than that: Remarque succeeded in transcending his own personal situation; he touched on a nerve of his time, reflecting the experiences of a whole generation of young men on whom the war had left an indelible mark. Remarque uses his own personal experiences in a similar fashion as the starting point for nearly all his subsequent novels. This exorcism of his own doubts and conflicts enabled him to make a huge step forward away from the preciosities of *Die Traumbude* and of the little prose and verse pieces penned for *Die Schönheit*.

Although the novel is divided into twelve chapters of varying length, they do not necessarily point to more than one facet of the basic structure of *Im Westen nichts Neues*. In this novel he is introducing a structural technique— which he was to refine in his subsequent works—which involves a series of small episodes as building bricks, not necessarily related to one another causally (that is to say, the "plot" is not particularly important), but cumulative in effect. Bäumer's account is very much like a diary, consisting in the main of either description of a sequence of events or internal monologue, without linking passages of any kind. It is, one might say, without seeking to over-stretch the comparison, a kind of "Stationenroman" on the lines of the Brechtian epic theatre with its "Stationendramen," that is, a novel held together, not by the traditional glue of a developing action culminating in a climax and denouement, but rather by broader thematic links, such as character or ideas. And, as far as Remarque's novels in general are concerned, there is a strange inverse relationship between their literary quality and the tightness of their plot.

Im Westen nichts Neues falls into three parts plus a contemplative interlude. The first part explores the experiences of the private soldier at the front and behind the lines, together with reflections back on home, the last days in school and life in the training barracks. It opens with a depleted company newly returned from the front, only eighty men out of a hundred and fifty, and concludes in similar vein with the return of another company, this time reduced to a mere thirty-two men. The central section deals partly with women (of whom a little more later), aspirations towards a world of love beyond the war, and partly with Bäumer's disastrous experience of leave, when he fails to regain contact with his past. There then follows a contemplative interlude, principally devoted to Bäumer's thoughts as he stands guard over a group of Russian prisoners of war; in this section, he actually ponders on the wider political and moral issues raised by the armed conflict (not a few critics must have had faulty copies of *Im Westen nichts Neues* with these particular pages expunged!). In the final section the action becomes more concentrated: vignettes of fellow soldiers, each ending in their death, are sandwiched between periods of reflection and contemplation, and the narrative technique—unusually for Remarque—switches over from blocks of description and action with a high content of dialogue to a summarized, compressed account of the concluding phase of the war, as time seems to become suspended and the comrades' emotions utterly numbered. And, at the end, Bäumer dies, just as peace is approaching.

Reading critics of *Im Westen nichts Neues*, one might all too readily gain the impression that the novel is a succession of nightmarish situations and unrelieved gloom, but this is far from being the case. Remarque skillfully paces the development of the action, interposing scenes of real happiness and contentment, some of which contain episodes that are extremely funny. On one such occasion, Bäumer clumsily attempts to "liberate" a brace of geese from a farmyard; he is cornered by the farm bulldog and pinned to the ground by that animal; and, finally, he manages to extricate his revolver:

> When I get my revolver in my hand, it starts to shake. I press my hand on to the ground and tell myself: raise the revolver, fire before the dog can get at me and make myself scarce. Slowly I take my breath and calm down. Then, holding my breath, I jerk the revolver into the air, it goes off, the dog leaps yowling to one side, I reach the stable door and go head over heels over one of the geese which had fled from me.

So he makes a grab for it, hurls it over the wall to Kat, who puts the bird out of its misery; and Bäumer joins them, having just escaped the fangs of the frustrated bulldog. (Almost as funny, but unintentionally so, is the National Socialist critic Nickl's accusation against Remarque that this is another instance of double standards: on the one hand, men protest violently against the sufferings of horses in warfare, but on the other they are quite prepared to kill and eat geese. Nickl must have been a vegetarian as well as a National Socialist)

Another amusing episode which is equally concerned with food, but this time, so to speak, from a different point of view, relates to the inevitable outcome of gastronomic excess. Kat manages to acquire two sucking pigs, and these are roasted with all the trimmings:

> We fall asleep chewing. But things get bad in the night. We have eaten too much fat. Fresh roast suckling pig has a devastating effect on the bowels. There is an incessant to-ing and fro-ing in the dugout. Men are squatting about outside in twos and threes with their trousers down, cursing. Getting on for four in the morning we achieve a record: all eleven men . . . on their haunches outside together.

Even the tyrannical corporal Himmelstoss gives occasion for some amusement, as when the soldiers obey his orders with excessive slowness, thus whipping him into a hoarse frenzy; but there is a grimmer side to the humour, too, both in the scene where Himmelstoss is swathed in a sheet and beaten by the vengeful group of comrades, and when their ex-teacher Kantorek is also humiliated by a former pupil of his in the barracks when the rôles are reversed and Kantorek is actually a subordinate to his erstwhile student.

Such episodes, however, are not scattered randomly about the novel; in this, as in all else, Remarque pays considerable attention to the detailed organization of his material. Opening on a positive note, the novel alternates light and dark episodes, the intensity of both increasing as the narrative progresses. In Chapter I, the comrades sit *al fresco* on latrine buckets in a circle playing cards in a scene of tranquil contentment; and this sequence is closely followed by a visit to the dying Kemmerich. Chapter V brings the *contretemps* with the goose, which is then consumed with considerable relish in an atmosphere of peace and fulfillment; and this comes just before the comrades move up to the front line past coffins piled high in readiness for the victims of the coming offensive. And, finally, in Chapter X there is a sequence in an evacuated village—"an idyll of guzzling and sleeping"—which they are suppose to be guarding, and where they have been left more or less to their own devices; and this is immediately followed by Bäumer and Kropp sustaining wounds in action. Each of the positive scenes, it will have been noted, is concerned with basic functions of the human body; and we shall be returning to this preoccupation with the essentials of life later.

Similarly, Remarque establishes a series of contrasts between scenes at the front and behind the lines, in an alternating sequence in which more and more stress comes to be placed on the front as the struggle becomes grimmer and the small group of comrades finds its numbers gradually whittled down. This aspect of the novel's structure is reflected in the chapter endings, each of which—with the exception of the Russian prisoners interlude in Chapter VIII—is concerned with a departure or a return of some kind, and the novel ends with the final departure from this life by Bäumer.

The process being depicted is one of a decreasing freedom of action and a growing sense of claustrophobia; there is, it becomes increasingly evident, no way out save through death. This relentless crushing of life and the closing in of death is underlined by the motif of Kemmerich's English flying boots. At the beginning of the novel, he lies dying, one leg amputated, and Müller is obsessed with the desire to inherit them. When Kemmerich realizes that he is close to death, he hands them over to Müller. When the latter dies in Chapter XI and Bäumer comes into their possession, we know that he too is marked for death. Of the original group of eight comrades, only one remains, Tjaden, and he in turn inherits the boots; but "Tjaden has luck as always" and he alone also will survive, despite the ill-fated boots, and indeed he reappears in the sequel *Der Weg zurück*.

The whole of *Im Westen nichts Neues* is in fact based on a series of antitheses which reflect various levels of alienation in the minds of the small and dwindling band of comrades. The first of these to come to light is that between "them" and "us":

> Whilst they were still writing and speechifying, we saw field hospitals and dying men;—whilst they were proclaiming service of the state as the highest good, we knew already that fear of death is the stronger. This did not turn us into rebels, deserters, or cowards—all these words came so readily to their lips—we loved our homeland just as much as they did, and we advanced bravely with every attack;—but . . . we had suddenly had our eyes opened. And we saw that of their world nothing remained.

There are two immediate consequences that flow from this gulf; the first is that the private soldiers form a closed and self-contained group, that is, they acquire and foster a sense of "comradeship" which dominates every aspect of their existence, but not in the meaning of the word coined by the National Socialists: this is not a case of the "Frontgemeinschaft" (brotherhood of the front) which is such a key concept in their interpretation of the rôle of the First World War, far from it. It is, rather, a negative state, a protective shrinking within a cocoon of intense intimacy with fellow soldiers as an essential means towards self-preservation and the maintenance of sanity in a world gone mad. After being lost for endless hours in No Man's Land, Bäumer hears the voices of his comrades who are out searching for him:

> An uncommon warmth flows through me all of a sudden. Those voices, those few, softly-spoken words, those footsteps in the trench to my rear suddenly wrench me out of the terrible isolation of the mortal fear to which I had all but succumbed. Those voices mean more to me than my life . . . they are the most powerful and protective thing that there can ever be: they are the voices of my comrades.

The second consequence of the gulf between "them" and "us" is that the comrades have lost all sense of belonging to that hierarchy of rôles that sustained them as they grew up: father, mother, schoolmaster and the rest have forfeited their validity; and a new hierarchy has come to be established within the confines of the closed group of comrades. In *Im Westen nichts Neues*, it is Kat, twice the age of the others, who acts out the rôle of the father: he is the source of authority, the leader, the indestructible one whose death by a stray piece of shrapnel as Bäumer is carrying him to a field station to have his wounds dressed so poignantly parallels the wasting away of Bäumer's disease-stricken mother at home. Parent substitute and "real" parent are now both irretrievably lost. (Of Bäumer's father we hear virtually nothing, save that he is a book-binder; and the French soldier Gérard Duval, whom Bäumer stabs in crater in No Man's Land, and who dies slowly and in great pain before his eyes, also followed that trade.)

Significantly, Kat's qualities are vastly different from those of the group's parents and other figures of authority: he is admired for his ability both to survive in a cruel environment and to care for the needs of his comrades. This finds its sharpest expression in relation to his skill at conjuring food and other necessities of life apparently out of empty air. And so it is hardly surprising to find Bäumer writing about Kat in these terms when he wakens in the night during a rest-break after a wire-laying party, frightened by a sudden sound:

> It is so strange, am I a child? . . . and then I recognize Katczinsky's silhouette. He is sitting there quietly, the old soldier . . . I sit upright: I feel strangely alone. It is good that Kat is there.

And again, as the captured goose is being roasted in the gathering gloom, Bäumer falls into a reverie and is roused by Kat:

> Is my face wet, and where am I? Kat stands before me, his giant shadow bent over me like home.

But, for Kat, as for the rest of them, "home" is the barracks; and the nostalgic reminiscences of the group are directed, not back at their schooldays and childhood, but towards their experiences in the training barracks, when, for example, the order was given for piano players to take two paces forward, and the unfortunates who did so were briskly marched off to the cookhouse for spud-bashing; or when Himmelstoss made them practise time and again what he evidently regarded as the difficult art of "changing trains in Löhne," which meant that they were obliged to crawl beneath their bed—which served to simulate the underpass at the station—and emerge smartly on the other side.

Thus a second area of alienation is on the temporal plane. The little group of comrades is effectively cut off from the past: "Since we have been here, our earlier life has been excluded from us, without our having done anything to bring that about." The years prior to the outbreak of war, and the values and knowledge which the comrades had acquired then have no meaning for them now. "Between today and the past there is a gulf . . . it is a different world." The past is an alien realm to which they could return only as strangers. It is as if the past has died; and, in order to underline this, Remarque twice employs the image of the photograph: when Kemmerich is expiring of his wounds in the hospital bed, he is described as looking blurred and indeterminate in outline, "like a photographic plate which has been double exposed," just a hazy shadow of the man he once was. And this image recurs when Bäumer is on guard duty in the darkness reflecting back on the scenes and experiences of his younger days and recognizes that, for him, they are irretrievably lost:

> It would be just like pondering over a photograph of a dead comrade; it is his features, it is his face, and the days we spent together would acquire a deceptive life in our memory, but it is not the thing itself.

In the front line, what they learned in school is utterly useless to them. At one point, the comrades joke about the knowledge they acquired in school, throwing the old questions at one another: "How many inhabitants has Melbourne?" "What were the goals of the Göttinger Hain?" (A circle of sentimental eighteenth-century poets.) "How many children has Charles the Bold?"

> We can't remember very much about all that rubbish. Nor has it been of any use to us. No one taught us in school how to light a cigarette under attack in the rain, how to make a fire with wet wood—or that the best place to thrust a bayonet is in the stomach, because it doesn't get stuck fast there like it does in the ribs.

On entering the army, they were thoroughly brainwashed into forgetting their previous scale of values, although these simply lay dormant at first; it was not until their exposure to front-line fighting over an extended period of time that they became obliterated altogether. In another example of Remarque's skillful use of theme and variation, the recruits were taught "that a polished button is more important than four volumes of Schopenhauer." This is then neatly stood on its head in the sequence where Bäumer is observing to his amusement his former schoolmaster Kantorek being drilled in the barracks square by his former pupil, Mittelstaedt, who cries out: "Landsturmmann Kantorek, is that what you call cleaning buttons? You never seem to learn. Unsatisfactory, Kantorek, unsatisfactory." He turns the schoolmaster's words against him, destroying all the man's values in a sour act of revenge for the fact that Kantorek, in encouraging his pupils to enlist, had caused precisely the same fate to befall them. This rupture with the past is one of the dominant themes of Remarque's work, the discontinuity of life, this jolting from one plane of existence to another for which man is completely unprepared.

Not only are they cut off from the past; a gulf also extends between them and the future. The inability of those who survive the war to readjust to peacetime conditions is suggested by the way in which Bäumer, walking along the streets of his home town while on leave, starts with fright at the screeching sound of the tramcars, mistaking the noise for that of a grenade whistling through the air. (The identical motif is repeated in *Der Weg zurück*.) The knowledge they have acquired in the trenches is as useless to them in time of peace as their school lessons in time of war.

Only those of the older generation, like Kat, will be able to slip back more or less unscarred into civilian life, since they came to war as mature adults, with a firm foundation in life, and they have something to build on when they return; Kat, for example, has his wife and, significantly, a young son to provide hope for the future. But, as Bäumer writes of his own generation: "The war has ruined us for everything." They have been caught up in the war when the hold of school and parents was slackening, but before they had had the opportunity to enter upon adult life: none are married, none have a job, none know which direction they want their future to take.

The young comrades feel equally alienated from the political and social issues of the day; it is not "their" war, and they can see no sense in the notion, say, of a nation actually wanting to attack another nation, a personification of abstractions which, to them, is nonsensical. And when the Kaiser himself appears to review the troops, their reaction is one of bemused disappointment; surely he cannot be the much-vaunted embodiment of he highest ideals of the German nation, they ask themselves; and this leads them on to challenge the whole question of the war, its origins and objectives. In the end, Albert Kropp speaks for them all when he bursts out: "It's better not to talk about all this nonsense at all."

Worse still, they feel cut off from reality itself and from their own humanity by the horrific routine of death and suffering in the trenches. They come to lose all sense of time,

> and all that keeps us going is the fact that there are even weaker
> . . . yet more helpless men who look up at us with wide-open eyes
> as gods who are able to for a while to evade death.

All they possess is life and freedom from injury. They have even lost all sense of their youthful vitality:

> Iron youth. Youth! None of us is more than twenty years old. But
> young? Youth? That's way back in the past. We are old men.

And in the trenches they are coming to discover that even life itself does not belong to them. At the very beginning of the novel, when Kemmerich is dying, it is stressed that the life has already drained out of him, that "the face already bears the alien lines" of death, that "there is no life pulsing under the skin any more," that he has the mark of death upon him. When Kemmerich has expired, Bäumer's reaction is one of terrible exultation, for he is alive, he has life within him, and he is filled with the most powerful desire to cling on to that elusive force whatever the cost:

> Streams of energy flow through the earth, surging up into me
> through the soles of my feet . . . My limbs move freely, I feel my
> joints strong . . . The night lives, I live. I feel a hunger, more
> powerful than for mere food.

The ground is frequently referred to in *Im Westen nichts Neues* as the source of a life-giving power, and the strength and significance of the "life force"—which has been conveniently overlooked by the critics—lies at the heart of all Remarque's mature work, and, as we shall see, it is a concept which he develops in the novels which follow upon *Im Westen nichts Neues*. One of them, *Der Funke Leben* (meaning: the spark of life) has the life force as its central theme, and the title of this novel, which explores the power of life in the midst of death and torture in the concentration camps, is prefigured in the scene where the goose is being roasted, and Bäumer describes Kat and himself as "two tiny sparks of life" in the darkness.

So when Bäumer and his comrades state that "we want to live at any price," the sentiments expressed have nothing to do with cowardice or selfishness. Running away from the fighting is never once contemplated as a possibility (the only exception being the farmer Detering, whose mind snaps when he catches sight of some cherry blossom which swamps him with recollections of his home). Life seems all the more precious when death is so close, but this does not cause them to falter when the call comes to attack the enemy. They fight like dangerous animals, but their adversary is not the French or the British—it is death itself, the negation of the life force:

> We are not hurling grenades against people, we are oblivious of
> all that at this moment, for there is Death in full cry against us.

This existence on the border of death causes them to concern themselves only with the basic essentials; and this is why the episodes of happiness we discussed earlier all concerned the basic physical needs of the comrades: food, defecation, sleep.

The one thing that keeps Remarque's characters determined to maintain their hold on life, even in the face of the most terrible injuries, or frightful tortures in *Der Funke Leben*, is hope; and when Bäumer confesses in the closing pages of *Im Westen nichts Neues* that "we are without hope," we know that his end is near. If, Bäumer acknowledges, the war had been over in 1916, it would have been possible for them to return to normality, but now they have been exposed to the front line for too long, they know nothing else any more, and in the words of one study of war fiction, "the front line has become the soldier's home, and it is best to die at home."

Despite all the critical assertions to the contrary, however, the comrades do not actively embrace their lives as savages, for perhaps the most tragic level of alienation which the novel explores is their separation from their true nature as human beings. When Bäumer comes out of the hospital ward where Kemmerich has just died of his wounds, he is filled, not with grief, but with an overwhelming longing, a hunger greater than that for mere sustenance could ever be, a burning desire to reach out and capture life itself.

Their adjustment to life at the front is more apparent than real; they adopt a deliberately superficial mode of existence, cutting themselves off from all emotion and passion in order to be able to survive at all. This causes them to yearn all the more intensely to be able once more to live as complete human beings. The goal of their aspirations is, however, far beyond their grasp: "It is unattainable, and we know it. It is as vain as the expectation of becoming a general."

When Bäumer returns home on leave, he recognizes that even those once attainable and modest aspirations which used to fill him—pursuing his studies, reading his books—have been driven out of him by the experience of war. The last words that Bäumer writes before he is killed reflect this loss of hope of ever returning to normality, although the life force within him will continue to "seek its way" for as long as he or others of his contemporaries are spared; and the use of the word "way" ("Weg" in German) forges the link with the title of the sequel *Der Weg zurück*, in which Bäumer's generation tries to find a way back to normality, even though the impossibility of the task is clear from the outset. The life force within them will struggle on, just as it now does in Bäumer, whether they will or no.

But the hardest lesson of all that the group of comrades is forced to learn in the war is that the ordered and meaningful pattern of life which they had once found in parents, home and school is a lost illusion; the causality which they had been taught was one cornerstone of their lives does not exist in the front line. There all life hangs on a sequence of blind chances, and chance is the only faith left to the soldier:

> The front is a cage in which you have to wait nervously for whatever is going to happen . . . When a shot comes towards me I may duck down, but that is all; where it strikes I can neither know exactly nor influence . . . Every soldier only remains alive by a thousand chances. And every soldier believes and trusts in chance.

The good do not necessarily prosper, nor do the bad meet their just deserts; in fact, the exact opposite seems to obtain. Joseph Behm, for example, a fat, contented lad, does not want to go to war, but lets himself be persuaded, for fear that he would have been branded a coward. Behm is one of the first to fall; wounded in the eyes, he rushes aimlessly about blind and crazed with pain, and is shot down before any of his comrades can reach him and bring him back to safety. Even the apparently indestructible Kat, who has a wife and son to return to, is killed by a tiny stray splinter of shrapnel.

The only apparent exception to this total disruption of causality is the fate of Himmelstoss, the corporal whose reign of terror over the comrades when they are undergoing their basic training culminates in his vicious treatment of Tjaden and another soldier. The two are bed-wetters, and he assigns them to a two-tier bunk, where each is to take turns at sleeping in the lower bunk. Vengeance for this and his other actions is meted out to him on the night before the trainees depart for the front line: Himmelstoss is caught as he returns from his favourite bar, covered in a sheet, tied up, and soundly beaten. When he subsequently appears behind the lines, Tjaden and Kropp insult him, but only receive token punishment when Tjaden explains in the orderly room about the bed-wetting episode. So in this case, it seems justice is done and seen to be done twice over; the wicked Himmelstoss does not profit from his evil ways, and later in the novel he is shown to be a reformed character; when one of the kitchen orderlies goes on leave, he puts Tjaden in charge of supplies and ensures that the rest of the group are assigned to three days on kitchen fatigue so that they get "the two things which the soldier needs to be happy: food and rest."

The semblance of causality in this sequence of events relating to Himmelstoss only serves to heighten the overall absence of causality from the principal strand of the action. And, if the Himmelstoss subplot is considered in the light of Remarque's later novels, it soon becomes evident that it really has little to do with causality as such; it is rather related to the motif of revenge which becomes so prominent in the novels of emigration, where the act of revenge is a protest against the absence of causality in a blindly cruel world.

Since the soldier lives by chance, all the skill and moral probity in the world are powerless to protect him against a falling shell or a stray bullet; and this situation is reflected in the structure of *Im Westen nichts Neues*, which has no real plot in the proper sense of the term at all, but operates instead on the basis of theme and variation, a sequence of antithetical patterns, and also of a highly developed substructure of recurrent images. We have already encountered the motif of the English flying boots and the photographic plate, but the most poignant of such motifs relates back to the days before the war; the two most important of these are butterflies and poplar trees. Like Remarque himself, Bäumer used to collect butterflies as a child, and when he returns home on leave he looks again at his collection, and reflects on the past which is now irretrievably lost:

> My mother is there, my sister is there, my case of butterflies there and the mahogany piano there—but I am not yet quite there . . . there's a veil, a gap between us.

Needless to say, the optimism expressed in the words "not yet quite there" is far from justified.

Earlier in the novel, this same gulf between the world beyond the trenches and the front line is underlined by a grotesque juxtaposition of two incidents, again in the context of the butterfly: two brimstone butterflies (in German, "Zitronenfalter," i.e. "lemon butterflies") flutter all morning over the trench in which the comrades are on duty, and rest for a while on the teeth of a skull. A few lines further on comes a description of a huddle of corpses after a grenade attack; two of them have literally been blown to pieces, and one

> rests his head in death on his chest in the trench, his face is lemon yellow, in his bearded mouth a cigarette is still glowing. It glows until it hisses out on his lips.

The colour of the butterflies is transferred to the face of the dead soldier, and their alighting on the skull's teeth is paralleled by the glowing cigarette on the lifeless lips.

The butterfly motif is taken up to very great effect in the film *All Quiet on the Western Front*; in its celebrated closing sequence, Bäumer's hand is seen reaching out to touch a butterfly, only to fall back limply in death as he is fatally wounded. In a parallel sequence in the novel, in which Detering is overwhelmed with a longing to return to the past, it is the delicate colour of cherry blossom which causes him to lose his reason. His comrades find him holding a twig of cherry blossom, and ask him why he has picked it. He replies that this is the time of year when his cherry orchard back home is transformed into a sea of white blossom; and so powerful is the pull of this recollection of past happiness that Detering simply disappears, presumably seeking to find his way back home. The comrades hear no more of him, but his fate is almost certainly that of the deserter: "For what do court martial judges a hundred kilometres behind the lines understand about that kind of thing?"

For Bäumer, the trenches represent the antithesis of the fragile, gentle and ever-present beauty of Nature, the "lost world of beauty," as Liedloff puts it. As far as Nature is concerned, Remarque never quite shakes off the sentimentality of his *Jugendstil* days. The butterfly and the cherry blossom symbolize the irrevocable disappearance of the comrades' past lives. Towards the end of the novel—it is the summer of 1918, and it is clear that the Germans have lost the war—Bäumer writes: "The days stand like angels in gold and blue, beyond our grasp, over the circle of destruction." Nature is totally detached from the conflict being acted out beneath.

Only once in the novel is there a reference to any military object as being pictorially attractive, and the circumstances are quite special: the comrades are waiting behind the lines for transport; it is a misty night, and there is a strange atmosphere of suspension from reality. A column of men goes past, but they are not like men, only a pattern of shapes against the gloom. And then more men pass, this time on horseback, but equally unreal: "The riders with their steel helmets look like knights of a past age; in some strange way it is beautiful and stirring." But, overwhelmingly, the war is bereft of all beauty; and it is significant that even the aspirant poet and dramatist Bäumer cannot share with an artist like Paul Nash a sense of awe at "these wonderful trenches at night, at dawn, at sundown." Nothing can compensate for the destructiveness and horror of this war, because it has cut them off from beauty and all that it represents. Nash may observe and paint with all the "inspired egotism of the artist who is sure of his vocation," but for Bäumer and his comrades such sublimation of the experiences of war is an impossibility.

Alongside the butterfly, poplar trees also represent the unattainability of the lost world; these are trees of Bäumer's home town along the Pappelallee (Poplar Avenue; the equivalent in Osnabrück is Am Pappelgraben, and poplars find frequent mention throughout Remarque's novels). There Bäumer and his schoolfriends used to catch sticklebacks in the brook running the length of the avenue, but it is all now no more than a golden memory of a hopelessly lost time. And, significantly, the sight and sound of the poplars occur again on the last page of the novel as symbolic of Bäumer's vain aspiration to find his way back to his past and to make use of the foundation laid in those early years to build himself a positive future.

Remarque also employs the repetition of certain key words, of which "Erde" (earth) and "Stille" (tranquillity) are the most significant, in order to express certain central concepts. We have already encountered "earth" as representing the source of the life force, of the energy that flows through Bäumer when he is overwhelmed by the recognition that he is alive, and Kemmerich dead; and, ultimately, it is to the earth that man finally returns. The notion of "tranquillity" is associated with the lost past, and in the last lines of the novel both these key terms are stressed once again: the day of Bäumer's death is "quiet and tranquil," and his body lies "as if in sleep on the earth."

Bäumer dies on one of those days in the final stages of the war when military activity is on such a relatively subdued level that the report from the front line states merely that all is quiet on the Western front. Death and suffering have become so routine that it requires a major offensive or a particularly gory occurrence to force the war back into the headlines.

As a result, language too is alienated, words are stripped of their true import, and the most horrific experiences are depicted in flat, matter-of-fact terms, just as in Kafka's chilling fantasies. Again and again, Bäumer admits the inadequacy of mere words such as attack, counter-attack, mines, gas, machine-guns and the rest to encompass the terrors they purport to describe. This does not only hold true for his experiences in the front line: when he is at home on leave, words also come to him only with great difficulty, and he finds that the words of his books fail to reach him anymore. He is unable to explain what things are like in action; and, when he pays a visit to Kemmerich's mother, he admits his total inability to put down on paper words adequate to depict the sufferings of the bereaved mother.

Bäumer's only recourse is to state quite baldly what happens when, for example, raw recruits—whom the comrades describe as children even though they are scarcely a few months younger than the majority of them—are dying under a gas attack, failing to take cover at the right moment, or going berserk with fear.

So everything is reduced to a numbing routine: in the descriptions of battle, of waiting behind the lines, thinking of home, enjoying the basic pleasures of food and sleep, the same formulae appear time and again to stress the sameness of every aspect of their lives, the treadmill of war from which there is no escape. Feeling and emotion dare not be allowed any room for expression, or insanity would inevitably result; and equally the words used describe the surface of the life to which they have been reduced, a string of bare utterances, an Expressionist sequence of substantives, as here:

> Grenades, gas clouds and flotillas of tanks—crushing, corrosion, death.
> Dysentery, influenza, typhus—throttling, incineration, death.
> Graves, field hospital, mass grave—no more possibilities exist.

This routine of suffering and the necessity for the suppression of feeling and emotion are to become a key motif in Remarque's later novels under the guise of the cliché.

The recurrent motifs that express the lives of the comrades also stress the basic essentials of the life to which their animal existence has reduced them. They concentrate, as we have seen, on food and defecation. Only fleeting reference is made to tobacco, although it is stressed as vital to the soldier, and there is also relatively little emphasis on alcohol, a state of affairs that is more than remedied in Remarque's subsequent novels. Surprisingly, perhaps, there is not very much in the way of references to sexual matters (especially for those who have read the reviewers and the critics rather than the novel itself). Early critics claimed that *Im Westen nichts Neues* was read by some for its questionable aspects, but it is far from being a rich stamping-ground for those in pursuit of titillation, even by the standards of the 1920's. There is little to cause linguistic offense, apart from references to a certain portion of the anatomy and its defacatory rôle, and there is no specific reference to details of the sexual act. There are a couple of allusions to adolescent curiosity about sex, and to Leer's fascination with girls from the officers' brothels, who are supposedly under orders to wear silk chemises and to bathe themselves before receiving visitors from the rank of captain upwards. The episode of the passionate Lewandowski in hospital has already been mentioned in the context of Remarque's supposed mendacity in relation to life in the military hospital where he was a patient with Peter Kropp; this is described in matter-of-fact-terms, as a basic element of life, rather than as an opportunity for obscene allusion or adolescent voyeurism. And the important sequence when some of the comrades cross the canal to visit the three Frenchwomen translates Bäumer's love-making with one of the girls into terms of the vague aspirations towards unattainable fulfillment which stalk the pages of his *Jugendstil* works. This comes across most forcibly when the comrades are gazing at a poster advertising an army theatrical performance, which portrays a man in a blue jacket and white trousers, and a girl who fascinates them, clad in a bright summer dress, white stockings and shoes, and holding a straw hat in one hand. They regard the girl as a "miracle" and their immediate reaction is to go off to have themselves deloused in a kind of ritual (as well as actual!) cleansing of their animal natures in response to such perfection and purity. When Bäumer embraces the French girl, he too is in search of a "miracle": "I press myself deeper into the arms which are holding me, perhaps a miracle will happen . . ." Similarly Bäumer is reluctant to climb into the bunk on the hospital train which is repatriating him, since it is made up with snow-white sheets.

But the miracle will never come; the comrades are either doomed to die, cut off from their former lives, from reality and even from their own true selves, or doomed to live on in a peacetime environment to which they will never be able properly to adjust, not least on the paradoxical grounds that, once an individual has existed for a period under the immediate threat of death, a return to "normal" life is an impossibility, since the senses have become so accustomed to being sharpened to the keenest edge by the experience of the front line that the comrades will in peacetime be in a constant state of frustration at the very lack of danger. So they and their generation are, in a very real sense of the term, spoiled for all time.

In all the debates about *Im Westen nichts Neues*, there is one common criticism made by defenders and detractors of the novel alike, from the National Socialists at one extreme, via the liberal pacifists in the middle, to the Marxists at the other end of the spectrum; and that is, that it does not succeed in providing a generally valid overall picture of the war. The novel's opponents argue that this one-sidedness constitutes a serious weakness in a work which has come to be regarded as official war history, its supporters on the other hand congratulate Remarque on refraining from spoon-feeding his readers, but instead assuming that they are sufficiently intelligent to make up their own minds about what happened in the trenches and to the rear. Interestingly, Remarque himself seems to fall into line with this view of *Im Westen nichts Neues*; in the Eggebrecht interview, he admits that he was seeking to do no more than simply put down on paper a "worm's eye view" of the war.

But to argue that Remarque is either a weak-kneed pacifist gnawing away at the nation's vitals, or a mature writer probing fearlessly at the heart of his generation's tragic fate, or again a bourgeois liberal who recognizes the disease and fails to point to a cure, is to miss the point entirely. Nor is it enough to indicate that the limitations of the work are attributable to the fact that Bäumer is a relatively unsophisticated young man who would in any event be incapable of comprehending the wider historical perspective into which his individual life fits. (There is, in any event, no inevitable correlation between the intelligence, insight or whatever of the author's mouthpiece and the quality or complexity of the narrative.)

The truth of the matter is that, in *Im Westen nichts Neues*, Remarque is proposing the view that human existence can no longer be regarded as having any ultimate meaning. Bäumer and his comrades cannot make sense of the world at large for the simple reason that it is no longer possible to do so, not just for this group of ordinary soldiers, but for a substantial proportion of his entire generation. Remarque refuses to lull his reader into a false sense of security, into thinking that God is in his heaven and all is right with the world—all that is amiss is that we as individuals are too limited in vision to be able to recognize the existence of a grand design. On the contrary, he demonstrates that the holocaust of the First World War has destroyed, not only any semblance of meaningfulness that the universe may seem to have possessed in the past, but that even the continuity of the individual existence has been shattered.

The largest unit of significance that remains is the individual life, sustained by the "life force" pulsing within, which holds the individual for the brief span of his existence and then releases him into death.

Philosophers, sociologists and all the rest may argue that this adherence to the notion of the "life principle" is a dangerous aberration and a distortion of all the received dogma of Western civilization; but this is how Remarque experienced life in the Great War with all its contradictions, pleasures and sufferings, and, fortunately for the reader, authors are under no obligation to construct internally consistent philosophical systems which conform to certain predetermined moral and ethical principles. It is for this reason, we would argue, that *Im Westen nichts Neues* captured the imagination of so many millions of readers, and why it continues to be one of the greatest bestsellers of all time. It refuses to inject a consoling but essentially illusory pattern of causality and meaningfulness into human existence.

Not only has the war destroyed any possibility for Bäumer and his like of reaching out beyond his individual existence and grasping at the myth of a meaningful universe, it has also shattered what was formerly a genuine reality, namely, the experience of a human life as a continuous single entity, an onward and upward progression through the years. Now even the individual life has lost its overall significance: it has become alienated from itself, and the knowledge and experiences gained at one stage are demonstrably inapplicable to the next phase. All that can be rescued from the tangle of the lives of Bäumer and his comrades is a profound desire to hold on to life itself, a blind instinct not to let slip the life force, and an equally blind hope for the future. As we have seen, when that hope fades in the closing sequence of the novel, Bäumer's end cannot be far distant. These themes are developed and explored further by Remarque in his subsequent works, especially in the two novels which deal with aspects of the Second World War; *Der Funke Leben* and *Zeit zu leben*, as will be seen when the time comes to discuss them in a later chapter. Nor is it coincidental that the word "Leben" (life) figures prominently in both titles.

Remarque's refusal to simulate meaning where he sees none is probably the cause of so many statements on the part of critics to the effect that *Im Westen nichts Neues* comes close "to being all things to all men"—which it certainly is not, unless "all things" include anathema and "all men" the Nazis. Behind such statements, however, there lies at least a partial recognition of the fact that Remarque has succeeded in distilling the common experience of ordinary individuals in the First World War and beyond, and that he has not set out with any false moralizing or philosophical preconceptions, but has sought honestly to convey his experience of life (and that of countless others), however unpleasant and negative his conclusions may be. Nor is he trying to seek refuge in any new dogma, or sidling towards any existing unorthodoxy, such as existentialism. Remarque is essentially a non-intellectual writer who prefers to express rather than to explain his experience of life, and in *Im Westen nichts Neues* he was able to come to terms with his own full realization of what the experiences of the war meant for him and for so many of his generation; this is why the novel was for him, and for so many others, an "Erlösung," a release.

In his excellent but solitary sturdy, Claude Cockburn defines as one of the qualities essential to a bestselling novel the presentation in an acceptable fictional form of "certain attitudes, prejudices, aspirations, etc., in the reader's conscious or subconscious mind." In this respect, as we have seen, *Im Westen nichts Neues* is remarkably successful. It is nonsense to assert, as the Marxist critic tends to do, that Remarque has become so totally identified with the "little man," the petty bourgeois, that he is incapable of objectivizing him. Anyone with a nodding acquaintanceship with Remarque's own predilection for the good life would hardly brand him as a defender of drab middle-class mediocrity. Remarque is simply being descriptive rather than prescriptive to borrow a turn of phrase from the grammarian; and his fictionalized emotional experiences were recognized by millions of people as something with which they had a great deal in common.

If *Im Westen nichts Neues* is regarded in this light, then questions like the accuracy of his presentation of the "lost generation" (the credit goes to Gertrude Stein for inventing the term) cease to seem so vital. It does not really matter that Remarque said that "our generation has grown up differently from any other before or since." Many a critic has pounced gleefully on this assertion with pronouncements like: "Ample evidence shows that the heroes of Remarque are not representative of a whole generation but only of a certain type." Remarque is not so lacking in perception as to be unaware of the truism, and it is disingenuous of his detractors to level this kind of accusation against him. What Remarque is asserting in his novel is that, so extreme were the experiences of Bäumer and his comrades that they were utterly devastated by their recognition of the discontinuity of life and the absence of any ultimate meaning in the universe. The majority of Remarque's readers, however, have not been eighteen-year-old front-line soldiers in the First World War; but they have, consciously or subconsciously, grown aware of a similar kind of insight in their own lives and experiences. As Cockburn suggests as a principle quality of the bestseller,

Remarque has given literary expression to attitudes widely felt by ordinary people at large.

This does not, of course, mean that everyone reads Remarque for the same reasons: just as the pit watched Shakespeare for the farce and the fighting, some of Remarque's readers may have scanned the novel for bloodthirsty battle scenes, the prurient passages (in which they will have been more than a little disappointed), its supposed political and sociological significance, and so on. None of these misreadings should be allowed to be taken as invalidating the novel itself, especially since so many have willfully distorted it and sought to reduce it to the level of a debating point in some campaign or other.

Cockburn stresses that it is not enough for the writer to touch on a nerve of his time; he must also write with consummate skill. In the words of Meyer:

> It is far more difficult to write a really absorbing book than to concoct a clever experimental one; it is far more difficult to tell a good story or to invent a memorable character that stays for a while in the human brain of millions or even of thousands than to fabricate *Kunstgewerbe* in the medium of words, so clever, so original that it can have any passing meaning we want to find there. This fashion will go, for it has come; and everything that is a fashion comes and goes, but the Odyssey has remained and so has Conan Doyle.

Meyer overstates the case, but that does not impair its validity; as we have seen already, Remarque constructs his novel with considerable skill, employing balanced episodes (happy and tragic alternate with almost excessive inevitability), recurrent motifs and other devices. There is no doubt that the style of *Im Westen nichts Neues* marks a substantial advance on Remarque's previous work, his *Jugendstil* writings as well as the rather indifferent journalism of his Continental days, and indeed it sets the pattern for the rest of his novels. Apart from the major techniques already discussed, there are a number of detailed stylistic devices employed by Remarque which all conspire to enhance the overall impact of the novel. Chief among these are the preference for similes rather than metaphors, which helps to highlight the latter when they appear at key points in the text; the emphatic use of inversion at the beginning of the sentence which, although a not uncommon phenomenon in German, is adopted by Remarque with particular effect at moments of emotional tension; his sparing but striking use of anaphora, which is most impressive in the sequence of short paragraphs each beginning "O mother" in which Bäumer reflects on his leave and his previous life; the tendency for concrete substantives to dominate at crisis moments; the occasional very long sentence contrasting strongly with the predominant pattern of short, simple sentences; and so on. In *Im Westen nichts Neues* there is no doubt that Remarque suddenly found his own stylistic voice, so to speak; the language is shorn of all but the occasional trace of his erstwhile sentimentality, and like most of his subsequent writing it is compulsively readable. Remarque owes his success as a writer almost as much to his stylistic craftmanship as to his ability to express in narrative terms the sentiments of millions of his contemporaries. From both aspects, the novel.

> satisfied a need, and expressed and realized emotions and attitudes to life which the buyers and borrowers did not find expressed elsewhere.

One of the worse fates that can befall a writer is to have a runaway bestseller with his first book; everything that follows will be held up against it, and sequels are notoriously disappointing. One critic at least has insisted—quite wrongly—that Remarque is a "one-book" author, despite the more than modest success of others of his works. Remarque did in fact regard *Im Westen nichts Neues* as his "first" novel—*Die Traumbude* he considered as part of his juvenilia and something of an embarrassment, and *Station am Horizont* as a journalistic exercise; in a letter to Rabe, he replies to the latter's invitation to come and give a lecture on his new novel in these terms:

> I have conned your arabesques with much amusement, but you will understand for all that, that at the moment I'd personally prefer to keep myself out of the limelight for a bit. It is only my first book, and one ought really to hide behind one's work for a while and only come to the surface if and when the second turns out good as well.

Remarque was determined to let *Im Westen nichts Neues* find its own feet; and, in refusing to be dragged into the publicity and controversy which surrounded it, he demonstrated considerable restraint and good sense.

There is no doubt that Remarque was more than a little overwhelmed by the reception accorded to *Im Westen nichts Neues*, and was determined to write a sequel which would not only explore the fate of those returning from the front line in search of a land fit for heroes to live in but which would also be a more substantial literary achievement.

ROLAND GARRETT

Liberal Education on the Western Front

The First World War fell like a thunderbolt on Europe, calling into question the highest cultural aims and ideals. Among its effects was a challenge to the ideal of civilized learning that had sustained and spread culture, a challenge to the foundations and justifications of education that, even though we have all answered it many times, we still find unsettling.

After decades of optimism, high promise, and exuberant international gamesmanship, the Western world stumbled into the greatest war it had ever seen. A series of threats and posturing, almost a series of accidents, led to a new form of warfare—immense ambiguity and hopelessness; an intensely fought stalemate, with a battle-line nearly stationary for three years (and German soldiers still occupying France at the time of surrender); a complete lack of decisive battles; and endless, routine slaughter of wave upon wave of soldiers as they attempted to advance through trenches and mud; the introduction of chemicals, tanks, and air power, the dehumanizing war machines of the twentieth century. The touchstones of traditional intellect and culture seemed to be like shadows or dreams, a tantalizing but frivolous entertainment whose irrelevance and lack of substance were demonstrated by the overpowering reality of the war. As Thomas Mann later wrote, the war was "the shock that fired the mine beneath the magic mountain."

From *The Journal of General Education* 31, no. 3 (Fall 1979). © 1979 The Pennsylvania State University.

The challenge to the concept of liberal education is reflected in the conversations and thoughts of front-line soldiers in Erich Maria Remarque's novel *All Quiet on the Western Front*. It occurs at a level we do not encounter much nowadays in our academic debates on vocationalism or the core curriculum. But its simplicity is engaging. And it remains powerful; indeed it reduces to an absurdity the argument we still hear for vocational relevance.

In the novel, a few school chums are together in the front lines of the German army and, during a brief respite from battle, think back to their time together in school. How many of their classmates are now dead and how many wounded? How many are now officers? What will life be like when we return home? In the terms of the novel, the return seems unimaginable, hopeless; but there is sudden humor in the recollection of the irrelevant questions that used to be asked in school. "What do you mean by the three-fold theme in *William Tell*?" one soldier asks suddenly, and roars with laughter. A series of quick, bantering questions follow, with no time or care for answers, in a spirited exchange of challenges that range across the several disciplines of knowledge in the liberal arts. What is the purpose of the Poetic League of Göttingen? How many children had Charles the Bold? When was the battle of Zama? What offices did Lycurgus consider the most important for the state? Does the pledge go "We Germans fear God and none else in the whole world"? Or "We, the Germans, fear God and—? How many inhabitants has Melbourne? ("How do you expect to succeed in life if you don't know that?" the narrator asks sharply.) What is meant by Cohesion? Irrelevant, laughable questions, the trivia of scholarship and liberal studies, like "those irregular French verbs with which afterwards we made so little headway in France."

Why irrelevant? Because they are all outside the war, which completely dominates. "We remember mighty little of all that rubbish [from school]. Anyway, it has never been the slightest use to us. At school nobody ever taught us how to light a cigarette in a storm of rain, nor how a fire could be made with wet wood—nor that it is best to stick a bayonet in the belly because there it doesn't get jammed, as it does in the ribs." Later, in a description of the shattered bodies in a hospital: "How senseless is everything that can ever be written, done, or thought, when such things are possible. It must be all lies and of no account when the culture of a thousand years could not prevent this stream of blood being poured out, these torture-chambers in their hundreds of thousands. A hospital alone shows what war is." What about the glorious advance of science and the human mind in that thousand years? This too is corrupted by the killing, we are told. "I see that the keenest brains of the world invent weapons and words to make it yet more refined and enduring." The challenge is a hard one, since, with all the advance of civilization, the suffering and sterility of war seemed to advance too, and to stifle the rest. One young soldier is hit on the field and his body quickly empties of blood; the novel reflects: "What use is it to him now that he was such a good mathematician at school?"

So that we will realize the depths of the challenge, the novel provides a powerful image of people without culture: dismembered corpses on the battlefield, entirely unclad, the men hit by mortars and blown clean out of their clothes. The title of the novel suggests too that the death was always with us, although we did not know it until the war. The German title is *Im Westen nichts Neues*, "Nothing New in the West," the phrase used by the army in the final lines of the book to report the stillness of the battlefield in one of the last days of the war, the day the narrator is killed. His death, "as though sleeping," the stillness of mind and culture, is "nothing new" to European civilization.

The vocationalist in our own debates on liberal education will insist on relevance—to job plans, to careers, to the leisure that is defined by contrast to paid work. War illustrates the weakness in this reasoning, for if relevance to human needs is the standard for education, why not recognize in our curriculum the needs of the soldier to know how to light a cigarette in a storm, or how to use a bayonet? In other words, the opportunity for work, careers, and pay is historically and psychologically conditioned. It already makes a host of assumptions, and not only about the future and the availability of certain kinds of life; it also assumes a meaningful framework in which life-choices are made. At the end of the interrogative banter of school-time questions, the narrator confesses to his friends that he cannot imagine what he will do should peace ever come. "All I do know," he says, "is that this business about professions and studies and salaries and so on—it makes me sick, it is and always was disgusting. I don't see anything at all. . . ." The critique of education is not simply that, however vocational it might be, it does not prepare one for war. Such a criterion could be set aside as an historical aberration based on the pessimism of the moment. The critique is more powerful: education does not prepare one for the reality of suffering and death; it does not help one adjust to and accept the human condition, which is concentrated but not foregone in war. Going up to the front, the soldiers pass a shelled schoolhouse with a row of at least a hundred new, unused coffins stacked along a wall. The soldiers know the coffins are for them; and the reader senses that education, liberal or vocational, is circumscribed and limited by death.

There is a larger perspective, however, for the novelist knows more than does the soldier. A soldier in the novel says simply that it is better that the war is in France, not in his own country, but that it would be better still to have no war at all. This blunt judgment terminates discussion, because the aspects of war understood by soldiers are limited. The national feeling of the soldier, Remarque says, "resolves itself into this—here he is. But that is the end of it; everything else he criticizes from his own practical point of view." So it is, I think, with the critique of education in the novel. From an individual, practical point of view, the educational system seems irrelevant. But more is possible, for the novelist's understanding is broader. And I believe that the novel reflects this situation, for the questions that seemed irrelevant are, on reflection, not really so. Moreover, the issues of ethics and human purpose that the novel explores go beyond the simple fact of death. The confrontation with death leads to questions and directions of thought that constitute a more complete, though still partial understanding of the human condition. If education can tie these fragments of knowledge together, it can illuminate both life and death.

Why does one person die and another live? Why do we have as enemies people we do not even know, and with whom we have no personal quarrel? Would there have been a war if the Kaiser had said No? How do we tell whether German professors or French professors are right about the war? What is it that wages war—the country, the people, or the state? These are questions asked by people in the novel. Thus are larger philosophical issues suggested, the issues of chance and decision in human life, the origins of conflict and loyalty, the extent of individual responsibility, the relativity of moral judgment, the social basis of historic movements. Although the ordinary soldier does not understand these things, and indeed an ordinary education may not raise these questions, issues such as these are a standard for education that the novelist does not abandon. They are important in war, like the use of a bayonet, but important outside war too.

The commitment of the novel is reflected in the miscellaneous questions that on first glance made the various disciplines of liberal education seem humorous and irrelevant:

—What is Cohesion? The question is not about the chemistry of Adhesion, how separate entities are held together, but about the force that binds together the different particles of a single unit. How are different things made into one? This question reflects social and psychological problems in the novel arising from the conflict between social atomization and unified social action.

—What about the three-fold theme in *William Tell*? The legend of Tell is largely about social unity, the conflict between people and their rulers, and rebellion against oppressive authority. In Swiss history it marked the unification of the three cantons of Schwyz, Uri, and Unterwalden, and the beginning of a new nation. In Schiller's play, moreover, three plots—those of the folk, the nobles, and Tell himself—are combined into a single story.

—The number of inhabitants of Melbourne? The population of Melbourne happened to be about the same as the number of Australians who died in the war, as a nation directly on the other end of the globe became a vigorous opponent of Germany, indeed with a casualty percentage the highest of all the British forces in the war; a vigorous opponent of Germany too in the rhetoric and humiliation of Versailles. The war showed that we are one world, interdependent, at least in conflict.

—The Poetic League of Göttingen? A group of young men who were poets rather than soldiers, given over to feeling and subjectivity, celebrating peasant and provincial life in simple lyrics and ballads; a quiet, primitive version of nationalism in German life in the early phase of "Storm and Stress," not unconnected with, though not yet absorbed into the spiritual turbulence of German romanticism, let alone the political nationalism of 1914.

—Lycurgus? The legendary creator of the constitution of ancient Sparta, who unified the state in a strict military organization supported by an elaborately defined and rigid system of education as well as a decisive subordination of the individual in the political order. The powerful council of senators he is said to have created served as a stabilizing force in conflicts between kings and people, and the simple, clean efficiency of the Spartan military state has been a utopian model since the ancient Greek defeat of the immense invading army from Persia

—The number of children of Charles the Bold? Insignificant, perhaps, until we realize that Charles, the last reigning duke of Burgundy, ruled a string of territories—from Flanders and Holland in the north, and Luxembourg in the east, to Burgundy in the south—that surrounded the great battlefields of the Western Front; and that Charles himself, famed for his bravery in war, died ignominiously in a ditch after an unsuccessful battle in Lorraine, his body mutilated and barely recognizable. Thus, in a sense, the children of Charles the Bold, are all those who died in the trenches in the First World War.

—The battle of Zama? In 202 b.c., Scipio and Hannibal met near the village of Zama, outside Carthage, and fought the battle that ended the Second Punic War. Liddell Hart, master historian of our own World Wars, wrote a military biography of Scipio that included a summary of the meeting of the two ancient generals and the significance of Zama:

> Livey prefaces the account of the interview [between the two generals before the battle] with the remark that here met "the greatest generals not only of their own times, but of any to be found in the records of preceding ages. . . ."—a verdict with

which many students of military history will be inclined to agree, and even to extend the scope of the judgment another two thousand years. . . . Scan the records of time and we cannot find another decisive battle where two great generals gave of their best. Arbela, Cannae, Pharsalus, Breitenfeld, Blenhiem, Leuthen, Austerlitz, Jena, Waterloo, Sedan—all were marred by fumbling or ignorance on one side or the other.

Liddell Hart entitled his book on Scipio *A Greater than Napoleon*; and a recent encyclopedia of military history notes that Hannibal's leadership, skill, and accomplishments "have prompted many historians and military theorists to rank him as the greatest general of history." Evidently Zama is referred to in the novel as an ideal, classical form of military leadership and decisive victory, contrasting with the fumbling, ignorance, and stalemate of the Western Front.

What can come out of the war? Again and again, in the novel the soldiers say ignorance and hopelessness. But there are other moments too. When the narrator, briefly home on leave, sees some docile Russian prisoners of war, he wonders at the ease with which, when government leaders whom we do not know sign some official documents, such quiet, childlike people become our enemies. This sort of curiosity he finds frightening and cannot sustain in the war. But the narrator vows that he will return later to these reflections, for they now represent, as an alternative to and an outcome of war, the only possibility of a meaningful existence. "I will not lose these thoughts, I will keep them, shut them away until the war is ended. My heart beats fast; this is the aim, the great, the sole aim, that I have thought of in the trenches; . . . this is a task that will make life afterward worthy of these hideous years." His story, like the war, ends in death, but the novel he leaves transcends it. A few cigarettes given to unknown Russian prisoners; a few momentous philosophical questions raised for us. This is the stuff of an education that is truly humane and liberal. The miscellany of teachers, pupils, scholarly disciplines, and facts; the empty school-house surrounded by coffins; can be given a significant purpose if made coherent by the right questions and sensibilities. The challenge of the war to culture and education would thus be met by these institutions on their own ground. The problems are not ever solved, but they are not intractable. And they are raised to a different level, where the broadest life-concepts, not simply bayonets and occupational choices, have the greatest significance.

HANS WAGENER

All Quiet on the Western Front—*A New Direction*

In 1928 Remarque felt depressed in his situation as the editor of *Sport im Bild*. As he stated in an interview, he realized that the reason for this depression and feeling of desperation was his war experience, and he observed similar feelings in his friends and acquaintances. He thus sat down and wrote *All Quiet on the Western Front* as a therapeutic attempt to rid himself of these feelings. He began writing after returning home from his office one evening, and finished the book within a period of six weeks.

It is difficult to summarize the plot of *All Quiet on the Western Front* in terms of one logical story line, since Remarque intends to describe neither a linearly developing action nor a psychological development. He wishes instead to characterize the condition of being at war. He also describes the state of being estranged from everything that one's former life and home represented. Consequently this novel consists of a number of short episodes that describe typical war experiences such as food disbursements, artillery barrages, gas attacks, furloughs, watch guards, patrols, visits to a comrade in the army hospital, rats, latrines, and so on. The story is told in the first person except for the final paragraph, where an anonymous narrator is introduced who reports Paul Bäumer's death. The novel in its original version is only 288 pages long and consists of twelve relatively short chapters, each containing several episodes.

From *Understanding Erich Maria Remarque*. © 1991 University of South Carolina. (Original title: "*All Quiet on the Western Front* [*Im Westen nichts Neues*]")

Influenced by their patriotic teacher Kantorek, who during drill time gave the class long lectures, asking the young students in a moving voice: "Won't you join up, Comrades?," the young Paul Bäumer and his classmates volunteer to join the army during World War I. Their military boot camp training, headed by the vicious sergeant Himmelstoss, is a rude awakening. They are soon sent to the front, where they experience the gruesome reality of a war in the trenches with several somewhat older soldiers, including Bäumer's mentor Katczinsky (Kat). When Bäumer returns home during leave, he is unable to identify with the memories of his youth. Nor can he understand the patriotic enthusiasm of the older generation, including his father who wants proudly to show off his son as a hero. Consequently he is happy to go back to his comrades where he feels he belongs. During a patrol Bäumer stabs a Frenchman who jumps into the same shell crater where he is hiding, and he witnesses the Frenchman's slow, painful death. Later he is himself wounded and experiences the horrors of war in an army hospital. Back at the front, he sees his comrades die one by one, until he too is finally killed.

In *All Quiet on the Western Front* Remarque deals with the last two years of World War I from the perspective of the common soldier in the trenches. Although it is not a historical novel, does not mention battles by name or give their exact dates or geographical places, a knowledge of the political background of World War I and the postwar years is nevertheless essential for understanding the novel and its reception in Germany.

Germany had gone to war in 1914 on the side of Austria against Russia in the east and against France and England in the west. Germany's hope for a quick victory in France by marching through Belgium, thus violating its neutrality, had crumbled as early as 1914. The unsuccessful attacks of German volunteers in Flanders, particularly at Langemarck in the fall of 1914, had claimed many lives and brought the German advance to a halt. The war in the trenches had begun. Large offensives mounted in the following years had failed—the Germans could not break through the French lines, nor could the French and British troops break through the German lines. 1916 marked the year of two great battles—the Verdun offensive and the battle of the Somme. Both battles resulted in hundreds of thousands of casualties on both sides. In the latter battle, for instance, some fifty thousand English troops were killed or wounded in the first three days of battle. As a result, the German armies were severely depleted and ever younger recruits were drafted. Due to a British blockade the German people were starving. In order to break the blockade Germany escalated its submarine warfare. This in turn led, after the sinking of the *Lusitania*, which carried some American passengers but also war munitions, to the United States' intervention on April 2, 1917, on the side of the Allied Powers. From that point on, Germany had to fight against not only armies with superior manpower, including the fresh American troops that arrived in Europe, but also against an overwhelming advantage in the quantity and quality of war materials, medical and food supplies. An armistice between Germany/Austria and Russia was declared after the czar and his government were toppled in the 1917 Russian Revolution. This event ultimately resulted in the separate Peace of Brest-Litowsk (March 3, 1918).

The military relief gained from this peace at the eastern front came too late for Germany. Several German offensives in 1918 were to a large extent unsuccessful because temporary gains could not be exploited due to lack of reserves. Tanks, used by the Allied Powers since November 1917, were a modern weapon rare in the German army. After several successful French offensives the German front gave way. Germany had gone on the defensive, and it became clear that Germany could not win the war. Negotiations for an armistice resulted in the Allied insistence on terms Germany considered insulting, and as a result the German fleet was ordered to resume fighting. This order provoked a sailors' revolt on October 28, 1918, which quickly spread all over Germany. Workers' and soldiers' councils were elected locally and took power. The Bavarian king was forced to flee; Emperor William II abdicated and went into exile in the Netherlands. On November 11, 1918, an armistice was concluded and the Peace of Versailles was signed on June 18, 1919.

This summarizes the historical framework of *All Quiet on the Western Front*. However, Remarque rarely mentions any specific historical facts or geographical locations, thus making it easy for millions of readers to identify with the characters of the novel. At the same time, Remarque's vagueness makes it impossible to localize the events in any specific time or place. Remarque recounts only subjective individual experience, that is, those experiences that are generally excluded from official historiographies. Only in the second half of the novel does he allude to the fact that the war is coming to an end, and he specifically mentions that Bäumer "fell in October 1918," so that we roughly know that we are dealing with 1917–18.

Remarque prefaces his book with the following:

> This book is to be neither an accusation nor a confession, and least of all an adventure, for death is not an adventure to those who stand face to face with it. It will try simply to tell of a generation of men who, even though they may have escaped its shells, were destroyed by the war.

This statement is a key to understanding the author's intention in writing his book and to the novel's "message." Since the book is not intended to be an accusation, the author clearly states that he did not consciously wish to make any political statement, not even one advocating pacifism. The phrase "simply to tell" implies on the one hand that the book is going to relate mere facts. On the other hand, however, this phrase denies the wish to "confess." This denial can also be interpreted as Remarque's own denial that this novel is an exact autobiographical account of his war experiences. Although written as a first-person narrative, the book is a fictional work and not an autobiography. Paul Bäumer should not be confused with Remarque. Indeed, Remarque has stated in an interview that he himself experienced most of the things he is reporting here, but it is also true that many things he just heard from others, especially from his time in the Duisburg hospital, and through letters from his friends. Working as a sapper, Remarque was in an area that was exposed to enemy shelling—otherwise he could not have been wounded. However, we must not forget that he did not actually serve on the front line, nor did he ever participate in hand-to-hand combat or direct attacks or counterattacks. Thus, Remarque himself had experienced the war only from the perspective of a sapper and as a patient in an army hospital. Many other aspect of the book are in fact autobiographical, particularly the scenes about boot camp in the barracks, the camp on the moors, furlough, work as a sapper, getting wounded, and being in the army hospital. However, these autobiographical elements are carefully interwoven into a work of fiction. It is unfair to take the author to task for having deviated from his own biography, as many of his contemporary critics have done.

The second aspect of the statement that prefaces the novel is that he is reporting about a generation of men who were destroyed by the war even though they escaped its shells. What he is thus saying is that his report has a general application and validity; that he wants to report not about an individual but about a collective fate. Furthermore, he implies that he does not want to tell us about the war experiences of young people, at least not solely, but rather wishes to justify the inability of young people to successfully cope with life after war, that is, life during the Weimar Republic. Such an interpretation focuses not on the war itself but on the year 1928, the very year when Remarque was writing his novel. One may very well argue that he uses his war experience to justify his own lack of professional success after the war, his inability to choose a solid career, and particularly his initial lack of success as a writer immediately following the war years. There is no doubt that the notion of an entire generation ruined by war and unable to function contributed decisively to the book's success. Many readers were readily able to identify with the novel's heroes and found a ready-made justification for their own inability to cope with life during the Weimar years. The "lost generation" theme, coined by

American writer Gertrude Stein, also plays an important role in the work of Ernest Hemingway, as can be seen in the epigraph for *The Sun Also Rises* (1928).

A third theme of the novel is also alluded to; namely, that of survival in war. Remarque claims that any war survival will at best be a physical survival and can never be an emotional or psychological one.

In his very first chapter Remarque jumps into the war action: "We were at rest five miles behind the front," he states. Throughout the novel it is not always apparent from the immediate context whether "we" refers to the entire military unit or only to the narrator, Paul Bäumer, and his immediate group of friends—here the latter is more probable. His immediate friends include his former classmates from high school, Albert Kropp, Müller, and Leer, as well as some more mature friends—Tjaden, a locksmith; Haie Westhus, a peat cutter; Detering, a farmer; and the forty-year-old Stanislaus Katczinsky, called Kat. Remarque does not present these soldiers as complete, psychologically developed characters. In fact, each is merely characterized as having universal human qualities that appear as leit-motifs in the text: Tjaden is the biggest eater of the company; Kat has a sixth sense for danger, good food, and soft jobs; Haie Westhus continually has women on his mind; and Detering longs for his farm. Thus, these soldiers actually can be placed into two distinct groups: the former students and the somewhat older generation who had already had a job and usually a wife. When Remarque refers to the lost generation, he does not mean the older comrades who were already rooted in a profession or family of their own, but the students whose youth was cut short and ruined by the war. These students never had a career or wife, and have nothing to come back to after the war, nothing that would provide a secure place for them in society. Later, the term "generation" also applies to a broader group of all young people whose life was ruined by the war.

The group of friends presented by no means includes representatives of the entire society. Workers and representatives of the upper strata of society are missing. Sociologically speaking, the friends thus represent a homogenous group of members of the lower middle class, the class to which Remarque himself belonged.

In chapter 1, only 80 out of 150 men in the "Second Company" return back to the camp from the front lines. The remaining 80 soldiers are happy to receive food for 150 men. "Stomach" and "digestion" are repeatedly mentioned and become the two most important themes for the soldiers. One scene—left out of the earlier American editions—describes a soldier sitting in a latrine for two hours. This event is described as a recreational idyll where soldiers can talk and rest.

In a flashback Kantorek, the class's former teacher, is introduced. Kantorek had so indoctrinated the boys with his patriotic speeches that the entire class consequently volunteered to join the army. (Remarque himself was drafted and had not volunteered.) For Remarque, Kantorek is a representative of the thousands of well-meaning but misguided teachers in pre-World War I Germany who sent young men into the war while themselves staying home. In Remarque's opinion this is a clear indication of the short-comings of the older generation. Educators who were supposed to guide the younger generation into the world of adulthood, into the world of work, duty, culture, and progress, have failed. The youth's belief that their elders have greater insight and wisdom was shattered by their sight of the first war causalities. All that these teachers had taught them—their entire world—view crumbled during the first artillery barrage. Remarque stresses the fact that these young soldiers were not cowards. They are described as courageously advancing in each attack. They love their country, but have begun to see how they have been betrayed. They now see the old world as a façade, that their education had no practical application. They are not provided with the necessary spiritual, intellectual, and psychological tools to deal with the experience of war. Remarque's statements resound as a reproach to the older generation. It is important to note that Remarque also underscores the conservative virtues of soldierly courage and love for one's homeland. This resulted in some initial positive reviews of *All Quiet on the Western Front* in right-wing newspapers and magazines.

The small group of former students visit their former classmate Kemmerich in the field hospital. He has had one leg amputated and is dying. Müller is interested in a pair of soft leather British pilot's boots that Kemmerich will never be able to wear again. Kemmerich first refuses, but during a second visit, described in chapter 2, he asks the narrator to take the boots along for Müller. Already before the second visit the narrator interjects an extensive passage pointing out that simply because Müller wants to have Kemmerich's boots does not mean that he has less compassion for him than someone who does not dare think of it. If the boots would be of any use to Kemmerich, Müller would do anything to get hold of them for Kemmerich, but it is clear that Kemmerich will die soon. At the front line only the facts count. In this way Remarque demonstrates how conventional modes of behavior and thinking have been turned upside down by the war. Being a soldier means to forget about conventional emotions and behavior. These must be superseded by a pragmatic analysis of the situation at hand. The boots themselves also have symbolic significance. Müller, who now has the boots, is killed. They are then passed on to Tjaden, and after Tjaden is killed, to the narrator, Paul Bäumer, thus foreshadowing his death.

At the end of chapter 1 the narrator laments the loss of his youth: "Youth! We are none of us more than twenty years old. But young? Youth? That is long ago. We are old folk." The war has aged them before their time; it has deprived them of their youth.

The motif reappears at the beginning of chapter 2. The narrator points out that these soldiers have been cut off from their youth by underscoring the difference between the former students and the older soldiers. Because of their interests, professions, and families of their own, these older soldiers are more firmly rooted in their former lives and are able to return to and continue their lives. For them the war is just an interruption of their activities during times of peace. The students, on the other hand, do not know what the future will hold for them. A touch of pathos and sentimentality marks this section of the novel, a trait that unfortunately became much more pronounced in several of Remarque's later works.

After the scene with Kemmerich's boots, the narrator recalls the time when he and his classmates volunteered for the army full of idealized and romantic feelings about the war. He then bemoans their tough boot camp training, which required the denial of all idealistic values of their former education. However, he also admits that giving up their individual personalities was necessary to survive. The narrator thus indirectly supports the necessity of carrying out seemingly sadistic behavior in a wartime situation. After describing in detail the deliberate harassment by Sergeant Himmelstoss, he concludes: "We became hard, suspicious, pitiless, vicious, tough—and that was good; for these attributes had been entirely lacking in us. Had we gone into the trenches without this period of training most of us would certainly have gone mad. Only thus were we prepared for what awaited us." The sergeant's dehumanizing and depersonalizing viciousness may be described as a necessary element of survival in war, but the statement made remains an indirect comment on the nature of war itself.

The friends do not break apart; they "adapt," and a feeling of togetherness awakes in them. Remarque feels that this comradeship is the only positive thing that the war has produced. It is again something found in many war novels or, to be precise, in many novels about the front lines written by politically right-wing authors. However, closer analysis reveals that this comradeship also includes a readiness to help one's fellow comrade. This readiness to help, however, is deeply rooted in the will to survive, which is only possible with the reciprocated help of the other comrade.

After Kemmerich dies and Paul Bäumer leaves the hospital, a great, joyful feeling at simply being alive fills him. A feeling of lust for life overcomes him, and he seems to be getting this inner strength from the earth through the soles of his shoes: "The earth is streaming with forces which pour into me through the soles of my feet. . . . My limbs move supple, I feel my joints strong, I breathe the air deeply." Remarque often uses such contrasts; and here when describing this rapturous state, this frenzy of life that seizes the narrator, he describes a kind of biological vitalism typical of his time. This kind of life-cult permeates all of his work from the first to the very last.

In chapter 3 ever younger recruits are brought in to replenish the company and fill in the gaps created by the mounting number of casualties. The detested Himmelstoss comes to the front, and Paul Bäumer's friends take their revenge by beating him up one night. Marxist critics have often interpreted this as Remarque's own private revenge on the older generation. Many of Remarque's statements about war support this claim. Here in chapter 3 Kropp suggests that wars really ought to be fought by the state secretaries and generals dressed in swim trunks and armed only with sticks. Clearly Remarque is not a political person. There are no detailed plans for organized resistance, nor does he advocate a utopian socialist state.

The tendency to mythologize is also apparent in chapter 4, where the group is brought to the front to dig new trenches. The noises heard from the front awaken the soldiers' senses, electrifying them, and making them more alert. The front has an incredible power of attraction. The earth is envisioned as the protective force which gives the soldier shelter, taking him in and protecting him. The influence of the front forces the soldiers to regress by many thousands of years. They become animals with bestial instincts that are the sole means for survival. This too is testimony to the dehumanizing effect of war. However, it also becomes clear in the following that even Remarque is not insensitive to an aesthetic appreciation of war, as he describes the shining backs of the horses in the moonlight, the beauty of their movements, and the sparkling of their eyes. The horsemen with their steel helmets look to the narrator like knights from a time long past, a scene that appears somehow beautiful and touching to him:

> The backs of the horses shine in the moonlight, their movements are beautiful, they toss their heads, and their eyes gleam. The guns and the wagons float before the dim background of the moonlit landscape, the riders in their steel helmets resemble knights of a forgotten time; it is strangely beautiful and arresting.

Such passages are not very different from right-wing war novels. Such heroic descriptions of war are reminiscent of the German writer Ernst Jünger, who considered war a steel bath, a storm of steel that tests character and forges a new man.

Suddenly a massive artillery barrage not only scares the young recruits but also kills and injures many "screaming" horses in a horrifying scene. At the end of the episode the farmer Detering asks a rhetorical question about the horses' guilt and considers it the most horrible aspect of war that innocent animals are involved. This argument is designed to make the reader question the soldiers' own guilt and the reasons they "deserve" to be in the war. After another surprise attack, including a gas attack, the same argumentation is transferred to the young recruits and at the end Kat shakes his head saying: "Young innocents——."

In chapter 5, after discussing the news that Himmelstoss has been sent to the front line, the friends discuss life after the war. Although Haie Westhus first thinks about catching up on his sex life, he would ultimately like to stay in the army. The life of a sergeant seems more attractive to him than the hard life of a poor peat cutter. Army life in times of peace is described in almost idyllic terms. Tjaden insults Himmelstoss verbally, which results in several days' confinement for him. In this scene Remarque demonstrates that the rules governing the front line are very different from those governing the camp. In one conversation the friends mock the lessons they were taught in school, assignments that have no practical application in war. Connections to cultural values and traditions have disintegrated. They can no longer communicate with those who stayed at home, and the continuity of development from their childhood to their current stage in life has been lost. These former students do not know how they can possibly continue when the war is over. After their experience it is inconceivable to them that they could get accustomed to a professional career. This inability to imagine any meaningful future after the bigger-than-life experience of war is seen by Remarque as the experience of an entire generation represented by Paul Bäumer and his friends. They have been spoiled by war, he maintains, spoiled for everything in life. They have nothing to believe in any more except war, and they feel lost. This is the main theme of the novel. It clarifies the perspective from which it is written, although its logic is not completely consistent. Neither Paul Bäumer nor any of his friends have been psychologically shattered by the war. They are now able to see all the patriotic phrases of their teachers in perspective, and they realize that their book knowledge has no apparent application. However, they are not broken; they do not get the opportunity to prove that they are part of the lost generation because they are killed one by one. Instead, Remarque demonstrates a kind of quiet heroism, a heroism that was created perhaps for the wrong reasons. But it is nevertheless a kind of heroism through which these young men are proving themselves.

Although Remarque condemns Himmelstoss and his methods of preparing the recruits for war, he also points out the usefulness of his hard, repetitious drills. The company leader, Lieutenant Bertinck, is presented as a reasonable human being ("He is a decent fellow") who gives Tjaden only the minimum punishment for insubordination. "They used to tie us to a tree," Remarque comments, "but that is forbidden now. In many ways we are treated quite like men." This is perhaps one of the strongest indictments of the spirit of Prussian militarism. Here it is not the war that makes the soldiers regress by thousands of years, turning them into animals, but the militaristic spirit of those who do not consider soldiers human beings.

It is interesting to see that every time he describes an intense war scene, Remarque interjects scenes of soldiers resting in the camp, thus skillfully interspersing his novel with action and rest. In this case he even paints an idyllic picture of the soldiers in a manner reminiscent of picaresque novels. The soldiers are described stealing and frying a goose, eating it in a deserted shack, and sitting together surrounded by death. The final words of the chapter describe an emotional celebration of comradeship: "but by my side, stooping and angular, goes Kat, my comrade."

In chapter 6 the sight of coffins piled high announces a new offensive. Paul Bäumer philosophizes about the importance of coincidence as the sole reason for a soldier to survive. Such arguments, of course, nullify much of the rightist notions of manhood and bravery. If a soldier stays alive in a modern war only as the result of a coincidence, all personal bravery and heroism is for naught in the battle for survival. Remarque goes on to describe the effects of continued heavy artillery barrages, the crumbling trenches, young recruits going berserk, and the sequence of attack and counterattack. He describes how the soldiers turn into animals without personal enemies. It is death itself that they fight against full of rage. Fighting is not done out of patriotism or heroism, but purely out of a feeling of instinctive survival:

> We have become wild beasts. We do not fight, we defend ourselves against annihilation. It is not against men that we fling our bombs, what do we know of men in this moment when Death with hands and helmets is hunting us down. . . . We feel a mad anger. No longer do we lie helpless, waiting on the scaffold, we can destroy and kill, to save ourselves, to save ourselves and be revenged.

In sharp contrast to this desperate description is an idyllic vision of the hometown, as idealized by childhood memories. Remarque describes an alley of poplar trees and a brook which he recalls from his own town, Osnabrück. These poplar trees and the brook often appear in his novels. They signify the innocence and peace of a lost youth. Remarque again laments the impossibility to connect with the past after the experiencing of war and concludes: "I believe we are lost." Thus, the soldiers' situation is described as a life with no link to the innocence of youth. Their ability to conform to a regular, bourgeois life after the war has been destroyed by the war as well.

The fighting continues. It is disheartening to see the ill-trained recruits get wounded and killed because of their lack of experience. The lamentation about the lost youth is transferred directly to the front line in this passage by describing how the youth is now killed before the eyes of the "lost generation." In the course of these war activities Haie Westhus is killed. The mention of the trees changing color marks the passage of time: It is fall now, no year is given. This time the company of 150 has been reduced to a total of 32, thus indicating the severity of the losses in this advanced stage of the war.

Chapter 7 finds the rest of the company in the camp again. Food and rest are the two basic needs of a soldier. He can bear the horrors of war only when he does not think about them. And it is this condition of not thinking that also prevents reflection about the causes of war. Humor and obscenities, one might add, are weapons for survival. Remarque postpones the great discussions and arguments about the fundamental issues until after the war. To be sure, his remarks have a threatening tone, but he is so unclear, so uncertain about what he says, that his words admit his (or rather Paul Bäumer's) inability to clearly visualize the coming revolution, as he concludes this pensive interjection by declaring: "We shall have a purpose, and so we shall march, our dead comrades beside us, the years at the Front behind us:— against whom, against whom?"

Remarque provides variety in this otherwise unrelievedly grim story by introducing women. First he describes friends discussing a poster with a picture of a pretty, clean girl which is in stark contrast to the soldiers' dirty condition. The poster depicts a kind of utopian dream. Consequently they decide to get rid of their lice. But reality is different from the pictured dream. They cross a canal and meet for several nights with some French girls who feel sorry for the German boys and make love with them in return for army bread. This is an attempt to try to forget the reality of war, although Paul Bäumer comments that "a man dreams of a miracle and wakes up to loaves of bread." In war, Remarque is bitterly saying, even love is reduced to pragmatism. Love is something that belongs to the private sphere. Thus the uniforms and boots, the symbols of anything soldierly and thus also the war, must remain outside when they enter the French girls' house.

Then Bäumer is given seventeen days' leave, including three days for travel, and he uses them to return home. Many aspects of this visit home are clearly autobiographical. The town described resembles Remarque's hometown, Osnabrück. A glass box with butterflies Bäumer had collected as a boy hangs on the wall—just as in Remarque's own home. Bäumer has a close relationship with his mother in the text, while that to his father is more distanced, just like Remarque's own. Moreover, his father is identified as a bookbinder by trade and his mother is described as seriously ill, dying of cancer, just as in Remarque's case. During his military training Remarque himself received time off to visit his sick mother.

Bäumer's furlough is marked by unhappy personal experiences. When he fails to see an old major on the street, he is forced to go back and salute him according to military etiquette. Remarque tells his reader that at home the old traditions are still—for now—strictly adhered to, whereas the realities of war force different rules at the front. For a front-line soldier such formalities are petty harassment. The reality of the front and the dream world of those who have stayed at home are contrasted time and again. For Bäumer it is already an embarrassment that his father would prefer him to wear a uniform so that he could proudly present his heroic son to his acquaintances. For Bäumer such a demonstration would constitute a misrepresentation of the reality of war. His father would like him to relate his front-line experiences. Bäumer considers it dangerous to put his experiences into words for fear that they will take on a kind of reality with which he would be unable to cope. At this point, as elsewhere in the novel, he is afraid to acknowledge what is happening "out there" at the front. The experience of realization is simply too frightening and would itself threaten his life since it would take away from the act of mere survival.

His father also takes him aside and leads him to a table in the inn reserved for regular guests. Here the old generation still clings to patriotic phrases and unrealistic territorial claims in a war they expect Germany to win. The contrast between the military stalemate and the reality of dying at the front, on the one hand, and the official patriotic optimism of 1914 which has been preserved at home, on the other hand, once again becomes clear.

Bäumer must realize that he has changed under the impact of the war experience and that the world at home—once so familiar—now alienates him. It is this feeling of strangeness, a feeling of not belonging, an inability to connect with the past, be it with his mother's naïve concerns or the schoolboy's world, that prevails in this entire important episode. This feeling is most clearly symbolized by the old books Bäumer peruses on his bookshelf. These books represent the lost youth he mourns, the old quiet passions and wishes, the impatience of the future, and the lofty joy of the world of thought. They describe the spiritual and intellectual world which he has created for himself outside of school. However, the books are unable to bring back his youth or to melt the heavy, dead block of lead which has formed deep inside him. It is here that Bäumer realizes that his youth is past, that memories have been reduced to shadows, and that the presence of war has erased all that he considered beautiful.

Remarque has presented this experience of estrangement and loss with a certain quiet pathos and sentimentality. We must ask ourselves whether it is justified to blame this supposed loss of youth only on the war and whether the realization of these hard realities is not something every young person has to endure at the end of his teen-age life. Rather than allowing the individual to develop in the process of growing up, to allow him to slowly become conscious of the new reality of adulthood and the impossibility of realizing the dreams of puberty, the war accomplishes this through a kind of shock therapy. The maturing process is shown as a necessary development that everyone must go through, one that war does not allow.

A lighthearted picaresque interlude follows this reflective scene, as is often the case in the novel. While visiting his old classmate Mittelstaedt in the local army barracks, Bäumer sees at first hand how his old patriotic teacher Kantorek is being drilled for active duty. A friend of Bäumer's, also a former student, takes revenge on the teacher for former humiliations in the classroom. But serious overtones appear as well. Kantorek had coerced a student by the name of Joseph Behm to volunteer and this boy was consequently killed three months before he would have been drafted. Thus Remarque underscores the guilt of the older generation symbolized by the patriotic teacher Kantorek. Bäumer visits Behm's mother, assuring her that her son was indeed killed instantly, and when she insists, Bäumer even swears an oath that he died without suffering. Bäumer maintains that he himself would not come back from war if it were not true, which clearly foreshadows his ultimate death.

Before Bäumer goes back to the front, he must attend a military training course in the camp on the moors. Remarque interrupts the novel here with this chapter in order present a new, more human picture of the enemy. Here it is the Russian prisoners of war who are housed in an adjacent camp with very little to eat. Remarque characterizes them positively by describing them as having the faces of "meek, scolded St. Bernard dogs" or as having good farmers' faces. This description also implies that they should be threshing, reaping, and picking apples. In other words, by making these people soldiers, Remarque not only describes them as having been estranged from their usual surroundings, but he also juxtaposes their natural calling, which is producing food, killing and being killed. Nature and nurturing are overcome by death and murder. Bäumer does not see enemies in them, only human suffering. These human beings have been transformed into enemies by the signing of a document by some unknown person. Remarque's statement delineates a theory about the origin of wars as being simply a bureaucratic act that makes people into enemies who are not, thus emphasizing the idiocy of all wars. However, Bäumer does not want to think this thought through as yet; he saves it until the end of the war. The senselessness of war seems to him to be the invitation to a new life after the war, a task worthy of the many years of horror:

> I am frightened: I dare think this way no more. This way lies the abyss. It is not now the time; but I will not lose these thoughts, I will keep them, shut them away until the war is ended. My heart beats fast: this is the aim, the great, the sole aim, that I have thought of in the trenches; that I have looked for as the only possibility of existence after this annihilation of all human feeling; this is a task that will make life afterward worthy of these hideous years.

Unfortunately, Remarque once again fails to clearly formulate his idea. The reader must complete the notion himself in his own fight against the possibility of such wars occurring again. A clear pacifist statement is lacking, but it may easily be inferred by the reader. Still, this is one of the clearest statements in the book indicating that it was intended to be a pacifist novel.

Back at the front in chapter 9, Bäumer confesses that "this is where I belong," with his comrades. The emperor arrives to inspect the troops. New, better uniforms are temporarily handed out, and a discussion within the group about the origins of war follows. Although extremely simplistic—after all, the speakers are simple people—Remarque again underscores the insanity of war without, however, coming to any conclusions about its causes. The emperor supposedly did not really want war. Moreover, it is impossible to tell which side is justified. The Germans and French, it is said in the text, both believe that they are only defending their homeland, a view that is confirmed by the intellectuals on both sides. Wars originate because one country insults another (but then, how can one mountain insult another one?). During this war Germans fight against French whom they have never seen before: workers, artisans, and petty civil servants. The implication of these statements is that war does not make any logical sense. Detering comes to the conclusion: "There are other people back behind who profit by the war, that's certain." With these words Remarque seems to allude to a—very debatable—Marxist explanation that wars are waged for the benefit of the big industrialists. However, Remarque does not pursue this idea. Instead, he describes other possible reasons for war: the prestige and glory for the emperor and the generals, and the war as a kind of fever or disease.

The conclusion is, of course, that there is no such thing as a "better" or "worse" kind of war. Even more important is Remarque's statement: "The national feeling of the soldier resolves itself into this—here [i.e. at the front] he is. But that is the end of it; everything else from joining up onwards he criticizes from a practical point of view." The mere fact that Remarque does not have his characters realize any "good" reasons for a war also makes the book a pacifist one. The fact that the soldiers are not depicted as fighting from some patriotic feeling, but have been simply drafted and are fulfilling their duty without thinking, was to make the novel appear insulting to the political right wing of the late Weimar Republic. That Remarque does not pursue the potential Marxist argument about the causes of war similarly provoked criticism from the political left wing. Remarque cuts off the discussion by interjecting a statement by Albert: "The best thing is not to talk about the rotten business." Remarque was reproached by Marxists for not providing a positive perspective. His "heroes" do not want to think, nor do they wish to talk, about war. Perhaps to simple soldiers in their situation that is the way it was, but the fact is that Remarque sees war as accidental, not conditioned by conflicts and constellations of economic interest.

When Bäumer is sent out on patrol, he has an anxiety attack. Only the awareness that he is out there for his comrades whose voices he hears from afar in the trenches fills him with a feeling of warmth and tears him out of his deadly fear. It becomes clear again that he feels close to them because they suffer the same fears and they fear for their lives just as he does. Comradeship as described here then is not so much a love for individual persons as a feeling of community with those who are daily threatened by death.

Bäumer is surprised by a French attack. In a kind of reflex action he stabs the Frenchman who jumps into the shell crater in which he is hiding and witnesses the dying of the man whose death he is personally responsible for. This Frenchman too is addressed as comrade, as a human being, and Bäumer understands that he is just as much a poor devil as he and his comrades are. Bäumer must feel all the more akin to the Frenchman since the latter is a printer, closely related to his own father's profession. And he vows more clearly than anywhere else in the novel to fight "against this, that has struck us both down; from you, taken life—and from me—? Life also. I promise you, comrade. It shall never happen again." Remarque thus unequivocally confirms the pacifist message of his novel. But we must use caution. The wording is extremely imprecise; the statement is emotional.

Bäumer wants to fight against "this." He has never directly or clearly thought about the origins of the war, and he can therefore only advocate a fight without direction and a clear goal. Back with his friends, the experience is treated as less important than it was. They tell him that he was just together with the Frenchman for such a long time that the experience had such an enormous effect on him. This does not mean, however, that Remarque wants to discount Bäumer's previous feelings. Rather, he wants to demonstrate the numbing effect that war has. "After all, war is war." Even feelings of human compassion are annulled by the fight for survival.

After this high point in the action Remarque adds another idyllic scene, which he expressly terms "an idyll of eating and sleeping." Placed in charge of guarding a food supply depot, the comrades prepare an opulent meal, including roast suckling piglets. Several days later they must vacate the village, and Albert and Bäumer are wounded by shell fragments. The doctor in the field hospital who operates on Bäumer is described as sadistic; and after a train takes Bäumer to an army hospital, another doctor appears who uses the simple soldiers as guinea pigs to operate on their flat feet. Even here the simple soldiers are characterized as dependent and unable to resist the superior powers, in the same way they must obey their superiors at the front.

The suffering that Bäumer witnesses in the army hospital is another occasion for him to reflect on the nature of the war and it consequences. He thinks how senseless everything is that has ever been written, done, and thought if something as horrible as war is possible. Everything in the world must be a lie and without consequence if thousands of years of culture could not prevent these torrents of blood being spilled, could not prevent hundreds of thousands of these dungeons of torture (hospitals) to exist:

> I am young, I am twenty years old; yet I know nothing of life but despair, death, fear, and fatuous superficiality cast over an abyss of sorrow. I see how peoples are set against one another, and in silence, unknowingly, foolishly, obediently, innocently slay one another. I see that the keenest brains of the world invent weapons and words to make it yet more refined and enduring. And all men of my age, here and over there, throughout the world, see these things; all my generation is experiencing these things with me. What would our fathers do if we suddenly stood up and came before them and proffered our account? What do they expect of us if a time ever comes when the war is over? Through the years our business has been killing;—it was our first calling in life. Our knowledge of life is limited to death. What will happen afterwards? And what shall come out of us?

All the main themes of the novel may be summarized as follows: the senselessness of war; the collapse of the old value system of Western culture and its inability to prevent war; the involvement of the older generation in allowing the war to happen and driving the younger generation into war; the young draftees' lack of roots in society; the soldiers' fear with regard to the time spent in the war since they do not know what will become of them later; their fear of not being able to adjust to a normal life, to find their place in society in times of peace since all they know is death and killing. The themes of pacifism, of the senselessness of all wars, and of the lost generation are thus combined without any clear transition. In Remarque/Bäumer's mind one conditions the other.

As is often the case, this scene of serious reflection is followed by a humorous scene in which the severely wounded Lewandowski makes love to his visiting wife in the hospital bed while the others play a game of skat, a German card game, making sure that the nurses do not interrupt the lovemaking. It is not surprising that this scene was excluded in older American editions.

The end of the war is near. New transports arrive every day with the wounded from the front line; the makeshift dressings are made out of crepe paper: the German army is failing. Germany cannot even properly care for its wounded and dying soldiers any more. In a short monologue Bäumer relates events of the last few months. After a convalescent leave he is sent back to the front. The fact that his mother does not want to let him return foreshadows his impending death.

Chapter 11 continues the account of events in order to indicate that nothing has changed—the front always remains the same. The soldiers are not counting the weeks anymore. It was winter when Bäumer returned to the front line. Now the trees are green, marking the advent of spring, symbolizing hope for a new life. War has become a routine of going back and forth between the front line and the barracks. The soldiers have become dull in their acceptance of war, which now appears to them to be just another cause of death, like cancer or tuberculosis, flu or dysentery. The only difference is that here death occurs more frequently, in a greater number of ways, and in more horrible fashion.

The soldiers feel that together they have formed a brotherhood of comrades trying to survive in an arena of death. Each activity is reduced to a mere act of survival and is therefore restricted to that which is absolutely necessary. Anything else would be a waste of energy. This primitiveness, this regression to bestial behavior, also provides the means for survival, including emotional survival. Entirely in conformity with contemporary vitalism, Bäumer/Remarque then demonstrates the existence of an active life force that has adapted even to this form of reductionism. All other expressions of human emotions are dormant, as the only concern is that life is on a constant watch against the threat of death. Men have turned into animals in order to give them an instinctual weapon; they have become dull in order to prevent a breakdown in face of horrors. If they would give in to clear, conscious thinking, they would surely be unable to face their lives right now. And life has given them the sense of comradeship so that they can escape the abyss of loneliness and abandonment. Thus, once again Remarque emphasizes comradeship as a significant weapon in the soldiers' fight for survival.

This support system is, however, so fragile that it slowly begins to break down. Detering, the farmer, sees the twigs of a cherry tree in bloom and thinks of his farm at home. Without thinking, he deserts right into the arms of the military police. But what would court-martial judges know about his motivations? Detering is never heard of again. The old contrast between front-line experience and the barracks or back home is thus alluded to again. Berger is killed next while trying to save a messenger dog, another example of a lack of logical thinking as the breakdown of inner defenses begins. Müller is killed and Bäumer inherits his boots, although Tjaden was supposed to get them, which clearly indicates Bäumer's impending death.

At this point it has become abundantly clear that Germany cannot win the war. There are too many fresh English and American regiments on the other side, too much corned beef and white flour, and too many new cannons, too many airplanes. The new, ever younger German recruits are dying by the thousands because of lack of military training and experience.

Remarque stresses the heroism of the German soldiers in light of these problems, soldiers who attack time and again in spite of the fact that their front is falling apart: "Is it nothing that regiment after regiment returns again and again to the ever more hopeless struggle, that attack follows attack along the weakening, retreating, crumbling line?" This is one of the instances in which one could defend Remarque's position against the charges of defeatism and of having smeared the memory of the German soldier. The company leader, Lieutenant Bertinck, who is killed, is described as "one of those superb front-line officers who are in every hot place." Although Remarque takes great care to show that not all officers are bureaucratic and uncaring about their men, it is interesting that he chooses only the lieutenant, a front-line officer of the lowest rank, as deserving of this praise.

High ranking officers do not appear in Remarque's novel. Therefore, no reasons for military actions are given or questioned in any way. The group surrounding Bäumer is not a military unit but a unit of friends who simply carry out orders. Seemingly ordered around by anonymous forces, the soldiers have no clear aim. Since the military activities take place without any defined rhyme or reason, their motives themselves are also not questioned or criticized in any way. War is just a dirty, destructive, life-threatening force caused by negligent and stupid politicians. The mechanisms of war cannot be understood by the simple soldier. War is only experienced as a gigantic destructive force against which the soldier fights for survival. He is thus not so much fighting against an enemy as against the anonymous power of war itself—against death. Equating war with death becomes a most pronounced theme in the final section of the novel as the friends die one by one.

Remarque emphasizes that the German soldiers were "not beaten, because as soldiers we are better and more experienced; we are simply crushed and driven back by overwhelmingly superior forces." He thereby justifies the German defeat and exonerates the soldiers, many of whom, to be sure, would be among his readers. However, this justification does not mean that he subscribes to the right-wing argument that the German army had been stabbed in the back by politicians at home.

Kat is wounded, and Bäumer carries him back to the barracks. When he arrives at the field hospital, Bäumer discovers that Kat is dead, having been hit by a shell splinter in the head while Bäumer was carrying him.

The final chapter is only a little over two pages long. The theme of the lost generation, of the lost youth, and the somewhat pathetic conviction that they will perish, resounds again: "We will be superfluous even to ourselves, we will grow older, a few will adapt themselves, some others will merely submit, and most will be bewildered;—the years will pass by and in the end we shall fall into ruin." How can it be that youth is gone? Youth is something that Bäumer/Remarque describes as something soft that made their blood restless; it is something uncertain, bewildering, and yet to come; it represents a thousand faces of the future, the melody of dreams and books, the rustling and inkling of what women are all about. Remarque/Bäumer does not want to believe that all of this has been destroyed by artillery barrages, despair, and enlisted men's brothels. Life is still in his own hands and in his eyes.

Looking closely at this description of what lost youth represents, we find that on the one hand it is a yearning for things romantic, for something still to be found in books and thus not real but ideal; on the other hand it constitutes unrealistic expectations with regard to the future, a kind of fulfillment to be derived from a relationship with a woman, presupposing a romantic picture of women which is just as unrealistic. Remarque deplores the loss of innocence that he finds in youth, just as many other writers envision children as symbols for innocence. Clinging to such visions would mean clinging to illusions. To be sure, Remarque makes the aspect of inner destruction more profound by not giving his protagonist the ability to develop more specific ideas about the future and instead having him escape from reality into childhood dreams. On the other hand, we might argue that according to his own biography Remarque himself did not have any more precise ideas. We might also argue that it is not natural for this kind of dreaming to be cut short by the horrors of war. The natural growing process should have been allowed to be more gradual and kinder. However, it is logically just as unjustified to make the war responsible for a necessary maturing process. In his next novel Remarque was to say that education has a similarly negative effect on people. This opinion stems from a romantic notion of what man is supposed to be, a pathetic denial of the necessity of growing up, of adjusting to the realities of adulthood.

In the final two short paragraphs of the book a new narrator is introduced who reports Bäumer's death in a few words. Bäumer was killed in October 1918, on a day that was so quiet on the entire front line that the report in the daily war bulletin was reduced to a single sentence: "All quiet on the Western front." The irony is, of course, that if Bäumer was killed, it was not all quiet on the western front. Thus, Remarque stresses the impersonal character of the killing, the discrepancy between a military point of view and the actual suffering and dying of millions of soldiers, of individual human beings. The title of the book itself thus becomes an accusation, and the entire novel refutes the callous statement of its title: it is not true that it was all quiet on the western front (the literal translation of the German text is "nothing new in the west"). It is incidentally not true that Remarque used a standard phrase of the German army high command. But he did choose a phrase that summarized the cold exigencies of the military value system. This is, also incidentally, the first time in the book that a precise date is given, by reference to the historical daily war bulletin. By taking the change of seasons into consideration, it is possible thus to conclude that the action took place roughly between the summer of 1917 and October 1918.

Remarque does not reveal the identity of the new narrator who gives a seemingly objective report and thus creates a distance between Bäumer and the reader. Yet he does describe the expression on Bäumer's face when he was turned over—a tranquil expression of being almost satisfied that it turned out that way, which makes us believe that this narrator is really one of Bäumer's comrades.

Since the entire preceding narration was first-person narrative, and since Bäumer nowhere in his story explicitly implies that he is writing a diary, this conclusion of the novel does not logically follow from the lost-generation theme. Although Bäumer's death was foreshadowed in numerous ways, it occurs in contrast to the theme of the lost generation, that is, those soldiers, who had escaped the physical destruction of war and remained consequently lost in the society. Thus, the initial statement of the novel can not refer to Franz Bäumer but only to Remarque himself who made himself a spokesperson for the majority of his intended readers, former soldiers of World War I. Given Remarque's tremendous success as a writer, it seems almost ironic that this success is based on the prediction that war destroyed the generation he writes about and made it impossible for them to succeed in real life.

As is obvious from the above quotations, Remarque has tried to write in a simple nonliterary language. He is trying to imitate the normal spoken language of the German front-line soldier with all its repetitive formulas and filler expressions that often say very little, its drastic slang, metaphors and comparisons that often derive their crude humor from references to digestive bodily functions. He thus writes in a style that is the opposite of the Neo-romantic style he used in *Die Traumbude*; indeed, he consciously avoided the somewhat stilted and sophisticated language of literature and used expressions that at the time were considered not acceptable for a literary work of art. The fact that the text is replete with soldiers' jargon identifies the narrator as a simple soldier who speaks the language of the majority of the front-line soldiers. This language, which was so familiar to the majority of the novels' readers, comes across as honest because it does not have the ring of "literature." Remarque thus wants to create the impression that a simple soldier and not a professional writer is giving a truthful report about the war. Through his language the narrator clearly appears as the mouthpiece of millions of soldiers.

This realistic language, however, is often interrupted by soft, lyrical passages which are emotionally charged and which at the same time are reminiscent of the "old," Neo-romantic Remarque of *Die Traumbude* and his early poetry. The following passage may serve as an example:

> The parachute-lights shoot upwards—and I see a picture, a summer evening, I am in the cathedral cloister and look at the tall rose trees that bloom in the middle of the little cloister garden where the monks lie buried. Around the walls are the stone carvings of the Stations of the Cross. No one is there. A great quietness rules in this blossoming quadrangle, the sun lies warm on the heavy grey stones, I place my hand upon them and feel the warmth. At the right-hand corner the green cathedral spire ascends into the pale blue sky of the evening. Between the glowing columns of the cloister is the cool darkness that only churches have, and I stand there and wonder whether, when I am twenty, I shall have experienced the bewildering emotions of love.

The images conjured up in this passage are in stark contrast to the war environment which surrounds Bäumer at that time. At other times, however, similar imagery even serves to romanticize scenes of war. In the above passage it is designed to idealize the memories of early youth and peace in order to underscore the loss of youth brought about by the horrors of war. One might be tempted to criticize Remarque for shifting from one stylistic mode into another, but passages such as the above can easily be explained by attributing them to the former student Bäumer, who had literary ambitions and who was taken directly out of school to be trained as a murderer. Bäumer's education has not endowed him with the ability to rationally question the origin or purpose of war; it is rather the reason for his heightened sensibility.

Other passages that contain strong emotional outbursts and a pathos that seems to contradict the matter-of-factness of a soldier's life with its concentration on survival are like Expressionist prose poems with all their pathetic questioning—for example, the following, which is taken from one of the last pages of the book:

> Summer of 1918—Never has life in its niggardliness seemed to us so desirable as now;—the red poppies in the meadows round our billets, the smooth beetles on the blades of grass, the warm evening in the cool, dim rooms, the black, mysterious trees of the twilight, the stars and the flowing waters, dreams and long sleep——. O Life, life, life!
>
> Summer of 1918—Never was so much silently suffered as in the moment when we depart once again for the front line. Wild, tormenting rumours of an armistice and peace are in the air, they lay hold on our hearts and make the return to the front harder than ever.
>
> Summer of 1918—Never was life in the line more bitter and full of horror in the hours of the bombardment, when the blanched faces lie in the dirt and the hands clutch at the one thought: No! No! Not now! Not now at the last moment!
>
> Summer of 1918—Breath of hope that sweeps over the scorched fields, raging fever of impatience, of disappointment, of the most agonizing terror of death, insensate question: Why? Why do they not make an end? And why do these rumours of an end fly about?

The repetition of the phrase "Summer of 1918" marks the individual paragraphs off like stanzas of a poem. The repeated exclamations or rhetorical questions are just as characteristic for Expressionist poetry as its life pathos is for German literature at the turn of the century.

The fact that Remarque presents his novel in small episodes, also typical of all his future novels, made it particularly suitable for serialization. It was easily possible to interrupt the reading and pick it up again with another episode without losing track of the action. The individual episodes can be compared to sequences of a movie, and they considerably facilitated turning Remarque's novels into movies. The episodes that immediately follow each other are often in sharp contrast to each other. Action contrasts with episodes of rest and calm, surprising the reader, creating suspense and at the same time corresponding to the experience of war itself. They are like stones in a mosaic, which only taken together form a whole picture of war. They enable Remarque to highlight only a few experiences, the way they assume importance in the eyes of Bäumer, rather than painting a complete picture in long strokes. The fact that these episodes are only loosely connected or starkly contrasted underscores the fact that Remarque describes only the condition of being at war and not the personal development of his hero.

It is a myth that twelve to fifteen publishers rejected *All Quiet on the Western Front* before it was finally accepted by the publishing house of Ullstein. In point of fact the manuscript was first rejected by Samuel Fischer, the legendary head of Fischer Publishers, because he believed that nobody wanted to read about the war anymore; Fischer thought the war experience was something the German nation wanted to forget. Ullstein took a different view; the book was printed in the daily newspaper *Vossische Zeitung* as a serial. Ullstein kept another manuscript ready to substitute for it in case they had to stop printing the novel because of readers' reactions. The opposite happened. During the serialization, from November 10 through December 9, 1928, the *Vossische Zeitung* more than doubled its circulation. With the help of a skillfully launched advertising campaign the book became one of the greatest international successes in publishing history when it appeared in book form on January 31, 1929, under the imprint of the Ullstein Propyläen Verlag. The first edition of 30,000 copies had been printed in advance, and within two months 300,000 had been sold. On May 7, a half million, and after sixteen months a total of one million, copies were sold in Germany alone. For quite some time the publishing firm received orders for 6,000 to 7,000 copies daily. Within a short period of time the novel also became a best-seller abroad. By the end of 1929 it had been translated into twelve languages and a million and a half copies were sold. In the summer of 1930 approximately three million were sold. It is impossible to determine the total number of copies sold worldwide, but in 1952 the author estimated the number to be six million. Others estimated the total number to be twenty to thirty million copies in forty-five to fifty different languages, though more conservative estimates place the number at eight million copies in forty-five languages.

Apart from the publisher's advertising campaign the flood of letters received and published by newspapers and magazines, and the many reviews and articles which ranged from enthusiastic acceptance to total rejection, also contributed to the novel's commercial success. Especially outraged were many conservative groups who claimed that Remarque's characterization of the war was unpatriotic and defeatist. The author himself was also severely attacked. Remarque was said to be not thirty but fifty-five years old. Some claimed that his name was not Remarque but Kramer, Remark read backward and that he was not German but a French Jew, and had never served in the war—and certainly not on the front. In fascist Italy the book was forbidden as early as 1929, and in Germany it was publicly burned in 1933.

Why such uproar about one book? By writing *All Quiet on the Western Front*, Remarque had taken up events and issues the repercussions of which were still decisive in the political situation in Germany. Millions of people could identify with the soldiers' experiences in the novel and saw themselves as one of the characters. Millions were able to use the war as a scapegoat for their own lack of success, their inability to succeed in life. They could blame not their own shortcomings or the political and social situation of contemporary Germany, but the war. For others the war was a high point in their lives, and to see it described as a horrible fight for survival seemed to betray all their youthful patriotic ideals and the ideals of manhood and bravery to which they were clinging in the present. Rightwing political groups such as the Nazis had mythologized World War I and made it the cradle of the spirit of the new Germany which they were envisioning. For them any other view was abhorrent—an insult to the fearless, undefeated German soldier who had been stabbed in the back by his homeland, by those who had started the November 1918 revolution.

Remarque remained rather quiet in all of the public discussions about his book. He gave only a few interviews, in which he claimed that he never intended to write a political book nor one which claimed to make any social or religious statements. He only wanted to report about the individual feelings of a small group of soldiers, mostly former students, during the last two years of the war. Remarque's intention to remain neutral was to no avail. His book had become a political issue, against his will, immediately following its publication. As evidenced by the many different and at times even contradictory political statements in the book and by the superficiality of its argumentation, Remarque was surely not a politically minded person in

1928, and he had no idea that his novel would have such political implications. His protest against war was diffuse and unclear in the text; the war served only as a literary backdrop to the fight for survival of the group of former students and their friends. However, the novel became the testing ground for conflicting political forces within the late phase of the Weimar Republic. In their fight against the novel and particularly its tremendous success, the various groups of the nationalistic political Right had found a common enemy and were thus able to unite.

In contrast to the reception in Germany, the American reviews of *All Quiet on the Western Front* were all positive. The American reviewers did not have an ax to grind with an author who inherently pleaded for peace, equality, and brotherhood, and as a result they did not attack the author as a pacifist or a traitor to the German cause. This is why they dwelt less on the implied pacifist message of the book, concentrating more on its credibility and ability to convince on a purely human level. It seems as if the description of suffering had completely dominated all political and, to a certain extent, aesthetic considerations. The reviewers praised time and again the book's sincerity, simplicity, honesty, its lack of sentimentality, its realism and economy of style. They overlooked the redolent sentimentality and pathos in the theme of lost youth, and particularly in the scenes involving Paul Bäumer's furlough back home. Also typical of the American reviews were references to other war novels, including Henri Barbusse's *Le Feu* (*Under Fire*, 1916).

Although the American translation of *All Quiet on the Western Front* is no better or worse than most translations, *The New York Times* immediately raised the question of censorship. The president of Little, Brown, and Company, Alfred R. MacIntyre, gave the following explanation in a letter to the New Republic:

> When we read the English translation we knew that the book as it stood would offend some people by its frankness, and that under the Massachusetts law, which judges a book not as a whole but by as little as a single phrase, its sale would probably be stopped in Boston. . . . We decided, however, to take this risk, and did no more than delete three words having to do with the bodily functions. We then offered the book to the Book-of-the-Month-Club.

In addition to this minor change, however, three additional passages were left out in the American edition, two of which have been briefly mentioned above: first, several lines referring to the supposed obligation of girls in officers' brothels to wear silk blouses and to take a bath before entertaining guests from a captain upward; second, one dealing with the German soldiers enjoying sitting on latrines in a meadow and playing a game of cards; third, a scene in the army hospital in Duisburg where a convalescing soldier is having sex with his visiting wife. No censorship had taken place in the British hardcover edition published by Putnam's in 1929. It was not until 1975 that Little, Brown published a new edition based on the complete British edition of 1929. One must add, however, that a letter from Putnam's to Little, Brown and Company of March 21, 1929, had conveyed Remarque's permission "to do what, in your judgement, is in the best interest of the book." It is certain that had Little, Brown not agreed to the cuts, the important advance sale to the Book-of-the-Month-Club would not have materialized.

Remarque was not the first to write a novel about World War I. As is clear from a review that he had written about a number of other war novels, he was intimately familiar with the genre. He simply continued an existing literary trend and gave it a new direction. In doing so, he together with another German writer, Ludwig Renn, whose antiwar novel *Krieg* (War) had appeared in 1928, established a new type of war novel which was later to become popular: The events are reported consistently from the perspective of the simple soldier, and the focus of the action is the events that take place on the front line. All other elements connect directly to these events. Thus, the war novel was changed into a front-line novel, which during the following years was a style adopted by politically right-wing authors.

With regard to Remarque's own literary development *All Quiet* marks a turning point: With *All Quiet on the Western Front* he had found the basic theme for all his later literary works—life threatened by large, overbearing situations, whether they be political forces or deadly diseases. In all his future works the backgrounds change, but the basic underlying principle remains the same.

BRIAN O. MURDOCH

Die Front ist ein Käfig: Paul Bäumer's War

The war happens to Paul Bäumer. He finds himself hurled into it without time to think (the only classmate who shows reluctance is bullied nevertheless into joining up and is killed almost at once). The images he uses for the front line in particular are significant. It is a cage, or a whirlpool, threatening and inescapable. Indeed, war becomes an entity in itself, something outside, a disease; Heinrich Böll placed as a motto to his Second World War novel *Wo warst du, Adam?* a quotation from St-Exupéry's *Flight to Arras* which describers war not only as an ersatz-adventure rather than the real thing, but as a disease, like typhus, and so does Bäumer. This is of course linked with the responsibility question, but as far as Bäumer is concerned, war comes from outside himself and imposes its will upon him. War means death, and death is the real enemy. An enemy in the sense of someone fighting on the other side, someone whom Bäumer attacks because he wishes to attack, is not present. We hear of the English or of the French (with an allusion even to black soldiers, probably from Senegal), and of the Americans towards the end, but few enemy soldiers are ever seen, with the exception of Gérard Duval, the French poilu killed by Bäumer as a reflex action in a shell-hole in no-man's-land. It is noteworthy that almost the only French soldier to appear in person is given a name, a trade, even a family—Bäumer finds photographs in his paybook. This all goes towards the contrast between the

From *Remarque: Im Westen nichts Neues.* © 1995 University of Glasgow French and German Publications.

single incident in which Bäumer is forced to face a real person for a period
of time and the picture of the rest of the war, where the enemy is a concept
rather than a reality. In the Duval incident, the striking feature is not that
Bäumer kills him—he does so as a reflex action, almost—but that he is forced
to stay with the man for a period, and is thus confronted because of his
enforced proximity to the other man by the humanity of the soldiers on the
other side. Normally this is not the case, even though when he tells the story
of the incident later Bäumer himself comments that such a happening is
"nichts Neues." The killing of Duval is not really even hand-to-hand
fighting; the essence here is that it is too swift to admit of human
considerations. The men have in general become dangerous animals,
surviving themselves only because of their animal instincts:

> Käme dein Vater mit denen drüben, du würdest nicht zaudern,
> ihm eine Granate gegen die Brust zu werfen.

The soldiers are not fighting; they are defending themselves from
death. There is no recognition of the humanity, let alone the identity of the
conceptualised enemy, and it is this that makes the Duval incident so
effective. It is equally noticeable that Bäumer, on his return, is made to watch
a sniper at work, and the language is both anonymous and euphemistic, the
language of target-shooting, when really it is about killing. Watching him at
work brings Bäumer back to what has become normality, and thus to the
comfortingly circular thought that "Krieg ist Krieg." The incident persuades
Bäumer that the war is not—as it had seemed to him just before—about
individuals, and that the Duval incident was an aberration. The First World
War was, after all, the first time that refuge could be taken behind the
anonymity of the machine. It was the first mechanised war, and it gave the
opportunity of dissociation that has been a feature of all subsequent wars. A
cartoon during the Vietnam war, for example, showed a bomber in operation,
with one man saying, as the bombs fell: "Just pretend there's no one down
there." There are few visible enemies in *Im Westen nichts Neues* and at the
same time the soldiers do not want to be confronted with human enemies,
because that forces a different kind of thought. It is well worth noting that
one of the rare outspokenly pacifist statements in the work occurs in the
Duval scene, with Bäumer's (spoken)

> "Ich versprech es dir, Kamerad. Es darf nie wieder geschehen."

The main feature of the physical description of the war is precisely the
anonymity, and this, apart from the Duval incident, leads to the soldiers' view

of the war as an external and malevolent force against which they are passive,
the real essence of which is concealed still further in slang terms. The
grammatical forms are revealing:

Nun aber gab es am letzten Tage bei uns überrashcend viel
Langrohr und dicke Brocken . . .

Diese Nacht gibt es Kattun . . .

All this reinforces the worm's-eye-view approach, and there is no
indication in the work of the larger course of the war. It is only by following
slight indications of place and time that we may locate the novel on the
Flanders front. It is an irony that the armchair strategists encountered by
Bäumer when he returns on leave point out that he as an individual soldier
cannot understand the war as such. The whole exchange is of interest. First,
Bäumer is instructed that a breakthrough is necessary, to which Bäumer
responds

daß nach unsere Meinung ein Durchbruch unmöglich sie. Die
drüben häitten zuviel Reserven. Außerdem wäre der Krieg doch
anders, als man sich so denke.

But this is rejected by his interlocutor, who knows better:

. . . es kommt doch auf das Gesamte an. Und das können Sie
nicht so beurteilen. Sie sehen nur Ihren kleinen Abschnitt und
haben deshalb keine Übersicht . . . aber vor allem muß die
gegnerische Front in Flandern durchbrochen und dann von oben
aufgerollt werden.

The irony of the whole is double-edged: Bäumer as an individual
soldier can indeed only see his own section of the front, but still he is right
and the other man is wrong: Bäumer is aware that a breakthrough is
impossible all along the line, and his awareness, based on experience, points
up the whole question of strategy. Questions of strategy are not discussed
because in the First World War—as was perfectly clear to Remarque and
others by 1929 and as had been clear to many soldiers in the war itself—there
was very little by way of strategy altogether. It opened with the unsuccessful
Schlieffen plan, the pincer strategy proposed by a general who was dead
before the war started, and it developed into a war based on the principle of
attrition: sheer weight of numbers, it was thought, would prevail. It is, of

course, easy to simplify historical details with the benefit of hindsight, but
the attitudes of the generals in the First World War was itself simplistic, and
as history shows, the years of trench warfare in fact produced few results—no
territorial gains for a massive loss of life. For 1917–8, Paul Bäumer's war is
an entirely realistic one, borne out by comparable writings, documents and
indeed what we have by way of film. Its wastefulness was very much clearer
by 1929, but the absence of any political basis, of any military strategy, and
the presentation of war as a piece of social, rather than military history,
ensures that it has retained its relevance. The First World War remains
baffling in its origins and in its conduct, and thereby makes an anti-war point
in a general sense that much more clearly.

In some respects, Remarque's presentation of the war is restricted.
There are few officers visible, for example, although there are some, and they
share in the experiences of the men who are—as they point out themselves—
in the vast majority. One cook-sergeant and one corporal-instructor are
castigated, though the latter, Himmelstoß, in fact undergoes a change from
being transferred to the front, and shares the experiences of ordinary
soldiers. A home-based major who adopts a drill-hall attitude to Bäumer
when he meets him on leave is implicitly criticized, but beyond that the war
is a private's one, a majority war. Other officers are simply not shown.
Bäumer himself, however, goes through a range of typical experiences, from
initial (and brutal) training to service at the front, from leave to service in a
camp for Russian POWs, thus showing him another enemy in human form,
although he cannot really grasp that these gentle and defeated souls are really
his enemy; then from being wounded to hospitalisation, from hand-to-hand
fighting to the more usual passive state of being attacked and defending
himself against death itself as woods, villages, graveyards and trenches
themselves are destroyed by shellfire. The deliberately long-drawn-out sixth
chapter, which is set at the front, allows Bäumer to enumerate all the kinds
of bombardment; he does so by presenting a simple list, a technique that
Remarque permits him to employ on various occasions. The brief comment
attached serves as a summary, and relates to several similar passages later in
the work. Here we are shown

> Trommelfeuer, Sperrfeuer, Gardinenfeuer, Minen, Gas, Tanks,
> Maschinengewehre, Handgranaten—Worte, Worte, aber sie
> umfassen das Grauen der Welt.

Im Westen nichts Neues—like many of the Weimar anti-war novels, and
those in other languages as well—systematically demythologises the war,
removing a powerful mythology that hovers even around the slight

ambiguity in the term "Great War." Various myths arose during the war itself, and were perpetuated actively from the home fronts, and passively to an extent by the soldiers themselves in their reluctance to give full details, either for fear of upsetting, through a reluctance to show weakness, for fear of being disbelieved, or indeed through official proscription. Edlef Köppen sets as the ironic opening motto to his Weimar novel *Heeresbericht* a quotation from the *Oberzensurstelle* in 1915:

> Es ist nicht erwünscht, daß Darstellungen, die größere Abschnitte des Krieges umfassen, von Persönlichkeiten veröffentlicht werden, die nach Maßgabe ihrer Dienstellung und Erfahrung gar nicht imstande gewesen sein können, die Zusammenhänge überall richtig zu erfassen. Die Entsehung einer solchen Literatur würde in wieten Volkskreisen zu ganz einseitiger Beurteilung der Ereignisse führen.

By the end of the nineteen-twenties, of course, it was possible to combat the myths by presenting a picture of what the war was actually like, and, indeed, to make quite specific attacks on the way some of the myths were maintained at home. Köppen, in fact, does this systematically in his novel, in which the narrated experiences of a fictitious soldier are juxtaposed with actual documentation, newspaper reports and advertisements which offered a quite unreal picture of the soldiers' life to those at home. Bäumer even comments upon this himself at one point:

> Was in den Kreigzeitungen steht über den goldenen Humor der Truppen, die bereits Tänzchen arrangieren, wenn sie kaum aus dem Trommelfeuer zurück sind, ist großer Quatsch!

The soldiers retain a sense of humour not for its own sake, but "weil wir sonst kaputt gehen," and it is transitory. The propaganda of consistent high spirits in the trenches is a lie: "der Humor ist jeden Monat bitterer."

The principal myth of the First World War was that war itself could still be something heroic, that it could ennoble, and that there was such a thing as a *Heldentod*. Those not actually involved in the fighting were of course unaware that this war was quite unlike the relatively recent Boer War; and the earlier, but already mechanised American Civil War, which might have provided useful lessons, was too far away. The Franco-Prussian War of 1871 was certainly still in living memory, but its course was again very different. Accordingly, behind all the calls to King, Kaiser or country lay a presumption in the popular mind that the soldier was still primarily an individual man of action, able to make the choice of fighting bravely, thereby achieving either death or glory, the former outcome subsuming the latter in any case. Postcards produced by all the combatant countries showed the soldier marching (and indeed sometimes riding) forward, or perhaps making a bayonet charge as an individual; and if—as often—he is shown as wounded or even dying, then this is happening cleanly. Remarque (and others) removed this myth precisely by showing that the soldier was usually in no position to make choices of any description, that he was rarely fighting man against man and that death in battle, far from being a quasi-classical *Heldentod*, was anonymous and agonizing, and far more seriously, was not even the worst thing that could happen. Of course the war poets (in English in particular) had made the last point by showing the bitterness of the maimed soldier, but the effect of Remarque's novel is cumulative. It is always worth recalling the very obvious: that the common denominator of all wars is that they are predicated upon people being killed or maimed. In the relatively brief description of hand-to-hand fighting in chapter six soldiers are bayonetted in the back or have their faces smashed with a trenching-tool.

There are no heroic deaths in *Im Westen nichts Neues*, and this was the basis of one of the criticisms levelled against it. Indeed, it cannot be denied that the First World War did give opportunity for acts of individual heroism (though the massive scale of carnage can hardly be justified for that reason, as the proponents of the *Stahlbad* view of the war tried). Remarque, however, shows us death first in terms of broad attrition—Baumer's company has been reduced from one hundred and fifty to eighty men when the novel opens, and by the end of chapter six there are thirty-two left. We hear of (and sometimes are shown), more specifically, the loss of Bäumer's classmates, and we see in detail in the final chapters of the novel in particular (some, like Haie Westhus, are killed earlier on) the gradual loss of Bäumer's immediate group—a group composed of former classmates and others befriended in the army, and to whom we have been introduced in the course of the novel. The deaths are presented objectively, with few comments (and those sometimes ironic), and the pointlessness of the whole war is made clear. What is made clear is the lack of grounds for any of the individual deaths, as indeed for the attrition which happens outside the novel. No ground is won, no victories are claimed, and some of the deaths are literally accidents of war.

> Müller ist tot. Man hat ihm aus nächster Nähe eine Leuchtkugel in den Magen geschossen. Er lebte noch eine halbe Stunde bei vollem Verstande und furchtbaren Schmerzen.

Der gleiche Splitter hat noch die Kraft, Leer die Hüfte aufzureißen. Leer stöhnt und stemmt sich auf die Arme, er verblutet rasch, niemand kann ihm helfen . . . Was nützt es ihm nun, daß er in der Schule ein so guter Mathematiker war.

Bäumer carries the wounded Katczinsky back for medical treatment, but on the way he is hit again:

Kat hat, ohne daß ich es gemerkt habe, unterwegs einen Splitter in den Kopf bekommen. Nur ein kleines Loch ist da, es muß ein ganz geringer, verirrter Splitter gewesen sein. Aber er hat ausgereicht. Kat ist tot.

Other deaths described are as graphic, but are not linked with individuals. On one occasion "zwei werden so zerschmettert, daß Tjaden meint, man könne sie mit dem Löffel von der Grabenwand abkratzen." In another case a death is presented in some detail but without our ever seeing the dying soldier. Under fire, Bäumer reports that the wounded can usually be rescued from no-man's-land, but this is not always the case. Sometimes they simply have to listen to men dying:

Einen suchen wir vergeblich zwei Tage hindurch. Er muß auf dem Bauche liegen und sich nicht umdrehen können. Anders ist es nicht zu erklären, daß wir ihn nicht finden . . .

The soldiers analyze without expressed emotion what is wrong:

Kat meint, er hätte entweder eine Beckenzertrümmerung oder einen Wirbelsäulenschuß. Die Brust sei nicht verletzt, sonst besäße er nicht so viel Kraft zum Schreien . . .

The cries last for days, but the man cannot be found. Inducements are offered to anyone who can find him, but Bäumer comments that the promise of additional leave is hardly necessary, since the man's cries can hardly be borne. He is never found, but Bäumer and his fellows can follow every stage of the man's death, from his cries for help to his conversation in delirium with his wife and children, to his final and long-drawn-out death throes. The description takes up several full paragraphs, and the soldier himself is seen neither by the reader nor indeed by those in the novel. The repetition of horrible and anonymous death is a feature of the novel, and indeed, even after death the soldiers are not safe from the war. Two passages remain in the mind. One of the most famous passages in the novel, in the fourth chapter, shows us the soldiers under fire, and Bäumer and his colleagues find themselves in a recently established military burial ground; ironically, Bäumer has to take cover in a grave that has been opened up by the shellfire and disgorged its occupant, leaving the living soldier to shield himself from death by death:

> ich krieche nur noch tiefer unter den Sarg, er soll mich schützen,
> und wenn der Tod selber in ihm liegt.

A counterpart to this comes in the central sixth chapter, just after the passage described already in which an unknown soldier dies so slowly. Here, the dead cannot be retrieved, and are indeed buried by the shellfire; the description is again unemotionally laconic, and quite uncompromising:

> Die Tage sind heiß, und die Toten liegen unbeerdigt. Wir
> können sie nicht alle holen, wir wissen nicht, wohin wir mit
> ihnen sollen. Sie werden von den Granaten beerdigt. Manchen
> treiben die Bäuche auf wie Ballons. Sie zischen, rülpsen und
> bewegen sich. Das Gas rumort in ihnen.

In Bäumer's war, however, death is not the worst: "Erst das Lazarett zeigt, was Krieg ist." The novel takes us into the front-line hospital in the very first chapter of the work, to the bed of the dying Kemmerich, who has had a leg amputated. Kemmerich lives long enough for us to see the waste of a young life, of a young man who could now no longer fulfill his ambition of becoming a forester even were he to survive. But he will not survive. All the while the reader is reminded of the stench of carbolic, pus and sweat, and it is significant that Kemmerich does not die until the second chapter, when Bäumer again sits by his bedside in the suffocating atmosphere, waiting for his classmate to die. His thoughts link the recurrent idea of lost youth with the despair of waste; his despairing wish that the whole world should be led past the bedside is of course what Remarque effectively does, showing the readers for the first time in the novel a detail not of war, but of the real result of war. Even the history books do not always make clear that the results of war mean people dying as well as countries conquering:

> Franz Kemmerich sah beim Baden klein und schmal aus wie ein
> Kind. Da liegt er nun, weshalb nur? Man sollte die ganze Welt
> an diesem Bette vorbeifuhren und sagen: Das ist Franz

Kemmerich, neunzehneinhalb Jahre alt, er will nicht sterben. Laßt ihn nicht sterben!

Bäumer has just been thinking of how young and un-soldierly they all look when out of uniform, and here again he reminds us that this is not the heroic death of a professional soldier, but of a civilian who has been bullied or has been forced by circumstances or by history into a uniform. Critics of the novel who miss any explicit pacifism in the novel have failed to notice too, perhaps, the clear message of that "weshalb nur?"

A far fuller presentation of the results of war is found towards the end of the novel when Bäumer himself is wounded and finds himself in a hospital, taken there on a hospital train in which, with irony once again, he is mortally (tödlich) embarrassed when he has to explain to a nurse his need to go to the lavatory. The experience of the hospital itself, however leads him to the realisation that here is where the realities of war become clear. The point was made during and after the war, of course, in many places; Siegfried Sassoon's "Does it Matter?" and many poems by Wilfred Owen ("Disabled," "Mental Cases," "The Chances," "A Terre") make the point, but it needed reiterating by the end of the nineteen-twenties. A. M. Frey's *Die Pflasterkästen* and Adrienne Thomas' *Die Katrin wird Soldat* both expand the point made so clearly by Bäumer, but not only does Remarque allow Bäumer to experience the hospital, with some quasi-comic incidents to lighten an effect which might otherwise become unbearable, he also has him enumerate the effects of war:

> Im Stockwerk tiefer liegen Bauch- und Rückenmarkschüsse, Kopfschüsse und beiderseitig Amputierte. Rechts im Flügel Kieferschüsse, Gaskranke, Nasen-, Ohren- und Halsschüsse. Links im Flügel Blinde und Lungenschüsse, Beckenschüsse, Gelenkschüsse, Nierenschüsse, Hodenschüsse, Magenschüsse. Man sieht hier erst, wo ein Mensch überall getroffen werden kann.

The generalising comment following the piling-up of different kinds of wounds is not yet an overt criticism, but Bäumer in fact goes on to describe in more detail still further effects of war—deaths through tetanus, shattered limbs the seriousness of which is made clear to him when he is shown x-ray photographs—and all this leads him to his conclusion, not only that the hospital makes clear what war is about, but that

> dies nur ein einziges Lazarett [ist], nur eine einzige Station— es gibt Hunderttausende in Frankreich, Hunderttausende in Rußland.

And it is this thought which leads the fictitious soldier Bäumer close to private despair in 1918, with a statement that made clear to the Weimar audience that the Great War had been a massive waste of life and that a new war would be the same, and to later audiences that war in general is to be condemned:

> Wie sinnlos ist alles, was je geschrieben, getan, gedacht wurde, wenn so etwas möglich ist? Es muß alles gelogen und belanglos sein, wenn die Kultur von Jahrtausenden nicht einmal verhindern konnte, daß diese Ströme von Blut vergossen wurden, daß diese Kerker der Qualen zu Hunderttausenden existieren.

The world "Kultur" is a key one; the war was described—on British medals—as "the Great War for Civilisation," and in German, emphasis was laid upon the defence of "Kultur," a word adopted mockingly in English writing to imply barbarism. Here, however, the war is seen not as a struggle for, but as a denial of civilization.

Death, often extended and certainly horrible, and a huge variety of woundings and mutilations, then, are seen as the main result and primary reality of the war. Given that the war itself is present throughout as an objective force, something which afflicts the soldiers and against which they are powerless, there are further short or long term effects. One of the terms that recurs is "Fronkoller," roughly equivalent to "shell-shock," but really summarising the extreme effects on the individual psyche of the situation of war. Partly it is immediate and quite comprehensible terror of the guns which causes this, and the case of Himmelstoß, when first under fire, illustrates the point. Another cause, however, is enforced inactivity; if the soldiers are passive rather than active vis-à-vis the war itself, they are frequently inactive even at the front, preferring a dangerous attack to the constant waiting, something which causes breakdowns and dangerous hysteria amongst the less experienced soldiers. Other attacks are brought on by individual events. These range from Kropp's impotent outburst at the end of the first chapter, after the visit to Kemmerich:

> "Verfluchte Scheiße, diese verfluchte Scheiße!"

to the case of the farmer Detering, disturbed first of all in the celebrated and memorable scene with the horses, the origins and impact of which have been commented upon widely, but the real force of which is threefold: the elemental agony of the beasts; the ironic impossibility of killing them, however strongly desired, because this will attract gunfire to them; and the effect on the countryman Detering. Later on in the novel it requires only a sprig of spring blossom for him to snap, and therefore (technically, at least) to desert, not however towards the neutral Netherlands, but towards his home, where he is quickly caught by the military police and presumably shot as a deserter.

All the soldiers suffer in the same way, their nerves affected increasingly as the war continues. Bäumer comments as a prelude to the desertion of Detering:

> Jeder Tag und jede Stunde, jede Granate und jeder Tote wetzen
> an diesem dünnen Halt, und die Jahre verschleißen ihn rasch. Ich
> sehe, wie er allmählich schon um mich herum niederbricht.

He himself is affected in a deeper fashion; he does not break, but new images of the war in the penultimate chapter bring him near to despair—the word "Verszweiflung" recurs. Bäumer's war has become increasingly a fight for his survival—which it always was—but against ever greater odds, as the German forces are affected by shortages exacerbated by the blockade, and as fresh American troops join the war. Its seeming endlessness and the inability of the men to envisage peace contrasts with the equally despairing cry in the summer of 1918 of "Nicht! Nicht jetzt im letzten Augenblick!" If Bäumer's war had been a cage and a whirlpool, and was perhaps typified by the frequent gas attacks, the inhuman and inescapable weapon, it now becomes a tank—the new weapons "verkörpern uns mehr als anderes das Grauen des Krieges." It is significant that the enemy soldiers, who are "Menschen wie wir," are completely invisible to them; all they can see is the embodiment of the war itself, these great machines that roll over them and crush them, impervious to their shells. The gas attacks could at least be countered with gasmasks. There is no escape from this new weapon, whose "Kettenbänder laufen endlos wie der Krieg . . . unaufhaltsam . . . unverwundbare . . . Stahltiere." The war has always had a profound spiritual effect on Bäumer and his fellows, making them subject to the laws of chance, of *Zufall*, to the philosophy of the "bullet with your name on it," which in its turn renders all other connexions void. At the end they—or more precisely Bäumer, the last of the immediate group—are spiritually bankrupt, unable to think beyond the war and beyond war itself. Bäumer's war is a lost one from the beginning.

By stripping Bäumer of all emotional resources and throwing him entirely upon the force of chance the war breaks him down mentally until he reaches the state of near-despair of the last chapter, a state of mind that resolves itself into a philosophy of acceptance of all that can follow simply because nothing could be worse. What the war does give Bäumer is a sense of strength in nature, in the unchanging earth to which he clings quite literally when under heavy shelling, and in the poplars and the rowans. But this is itself a kind of desperation, a grasping by the mind under impossible stresses at some kind of non-human constant. There is nothing else good that emerges from Bäumer's war, not even the vaunted comradeship, which is merely a defence mechanism, a fellowship in adversity which expresses itself in unified action, a state upon which military life always depends, even if here the bonding sometimes works against the very forces that have inculcated that fellowship. The communal attack on Himmelstoß is a case in point here, it is only a single incident and it has another more important significance than the expression of comradeship: it is the first expression of the violent solution of war having its reflection in the application of violent solutions to personal rather than national problems, a demonstration of what might be called original sin in man the war-maker. Bäumer, it is true, refers to comradeship as the best thing to come out of the war, but the comment has to be treated carefully. He has been talking about a feeling of solidarity engendered in the recruits whilst undergoing initial training, and developed in the field of battle. All this modifies the concept, and in any case, it is determined and conditioned by the war. Comradeship may be the best thing the war produced, but its temporary existence scarcely justifies the war. Indeed, throughout the novel it is not comradeship which is stressed, but loss: the gradual loss of all the classmates and friends. Comradeship in war is only one side of things; the other is the necessity of parting. Bäumer's use of the pronoun "wir" rarely implies a genuine closeness of relationship. An example of parting which is commented upon comes at the end of the hospitalisation scene, when Bäumer and Kropp have to part:

> Der Abschied von meinem Freunde Albert Kropp ist schwer. Aber man lenrnt das beim Kommiß mit der Zeit.

Only with Katzcinsky does Bäumer share a close relationship, and this is the product of chance rather than of a general comradeship born out of the war. Their relationship is close, but it is almost that of a father and a son. Kat the father-figure (something made clear in both film versions, incidentally), teaches Bäumer to survive, quite literally in the instructions about the different kinds of shell, and more generally in his ability to find food under adverse conditions; and survival against the real enemy—death—is a key theme, the one thing these schoolboy soldiers learn, and which replaces all the learning they have so pointlessly assimilated at school.

What really binds Bäumer and Kat is their lust for life, the fact that they are "zwei winzige Funken Leben" in the storm of chaos about them. And yet they both die. Bäumer's comments on comradeship are in fact developed at the end of the work, and here he links it with the solidarity felt by prisoners or the community feeling of those condemned to death:

Wir sind Soldaten und erst später auf eine sonderbare und verschämte Weise noch Einzelmenschen.

The comradeship is not an absolute; it depends—like the communal "wir"—upon their being soldiers. Take this away, and it is only natural that the feeling of community should go as well. It is no accident that Bäumer should in his last thoughts refer to his identity as an individual. War is concerned with the premature and abrupt killing of many individuals, and Bäumer, like all men, dies alone. Part of the message of the novel is that the war was not fought by the masses, by some kind of numerical abstract, but by huge numbers of individual solders. Much of the effect of the work depends on the fact that Bäumer is really the only character and that it is very much his war. Of course, his experiences were not unique, and as far as action goes, Remarque allows his characters to draw attention from time to time to the uniformity of the war; under fire in chapter six during the 1917 Ypres campaign, Kat comments that "es wird wie an der Somme" a year earlier. Many of the things that Bäumer goes through, sees, feels or thinks will have been known by real soldiers in the war (because Bäumer is, after all, a fictitious character). He himself is an individual, though, and that individuality should not be lost sight of: it expresses itself in his youthful sensitivity in showing us Bäumer's war, and Remarque's skill in making him do so in such a consistently convincing manner is considerable.

Chronology

1898	Born Erich Paul Remark on June 22 in Osnabrück, Germany to Peter Franz and Anna Maria Stallknecht Remark.
1915–16	Attends Catholic Teacher's College; drafted into the army in 1916.
1917	Sent to the front in World War I; hospitalized from serious shrapnel wounds in August; mother dies in September.
1918	Poetry is published in *Die Schönheit*, an avant-garde journal.
1919	Completes teacher training program and starts teaching.
1920	Publishes first novel, *The Dream Room*; stops teaching at end of year and works at a variety of odd jobs.
1925	Marries Jutta Ilse Zambona.
1927–28	*Station on the Horizon* serialized.
1928	*All Quiet on the Western Front* serialized in *Die Vossische Zeitung*.
1929	*All Quiet on the Western Front* published in book form.
1930	Divorced
1931	Publishes *The Road Back*, a sequel to *All Quiet on the Western Front*; *All Quiet on the Western Front* made into a film in the United States.
1933	Flees to Switzerland along with ex-wife when Nazis take over in Germany.
1937	*Three Comrades* published.
1938	Remarries ex-wife so she will not be forced to return to Germany
1939	Immigrates to United States.
1941	*Flotsam* published.

1943	Sister is beheaded by Nazis.
1946	*Arch of Triumph* published.
1947	Becomes U.S. citizen.
1952	*Spark of Life* published.
1954	*A Time to Love and a Time to Die* published.
1956	*The Black Obelisk* published.
1957	Divorced.
1958	Marries American film actress Paulette Goddard.
1961	Publishes *Heaven Has No Favorites* and *The Night in Lisbon*.
1970	Dies of heart failure in Locarno, Switzerland.
1971	*Shadows in Paradise* published.
1973	*Full Circle*, an adaptation of *The Last Station*, premieres.

Contributors

HAROLD BLOOM is Sterling Professor of the Humanities at Yale University and Henry W. and Albert A. Berg Professor of English at the New York University Graduate School. He is the author of over 20 books, including *Shelley's Mythmaking* (1959), *The Visionary Company* (1961), *Blake's Apocalypse* (1963), *Yeats* (1970), *A Map of Misreading* (1975), *Kabbalah and Criticism* (1975), *Agon: Toward a Theory of Revisionism* (1982), *The American Religion* (1992), *The Western Canon* (1994), and *Omens of Millennium: The Gnosis of Angels, Dreams, and Resurrection* (1996). *The Anxiety of Influence* (1973) sets forth Professor Bloom's provocative theory of the literary relationships between the great writers and their predecessors. His most recent books include *Shakespeare: The Invention of the Human*, a 1998 National Book Award finalist, and *How to Read and Why*, which was published in 2000. In 1999, Professor Bloom received the prestigious American Academy of Arts and Letters Gold Medal for Criticism.

WILLIAM K. PFEILER has taught at the University of Nebraska.

EDWIN M. MOSELEY (1916–1978) was Dean of the Faculty and Professor of English at Skidmore College at Saratoga Springs, N.Y. He has published fiction and criticism; his works include *Religion and Modern Literature: Essays in Theory and Criticism.*

HELMUT LIEDLOFF is the author, along with Jack R. Moeller, of the third annotated edition of *Deutsch Heute (German Today)*, part of a set for teachers.

WILHELM J. SCHWARZ has been professor of German literature at the Universite Laval in Quebec City, Quebec. He is the author of *Conversations with Peter Rosei*.

A. F. BANCE has been professor of German and head of the department at the University of Keele, Keele, England. He is the author of *The German Novel, 1945–1960*, as well as the author and editor of other works.

CHRISTINE R. BARKER most recently co-edited *Gender Perceptions and the Law*.

R. W. LAST has taught at Hull University. He is the editor of the *Modern German Authors* and *German Literature and Society* series.

ROLAND GARRETT has been Associate Professor of Philosophy and Chairman of the Division of Arts and Sciences at Indiana University at South Bend.

HANS WAGENER is Professor of Germanic Languages at the University of Southern California at Los Angeles. He has published numerous articles and books about seventeenth- and twentieth-century German literature.

BRIAN O. MURDOCH is Professor of German at the University of Stirling in Scotland. He has translated *All Quiet on the Western Front* and has written and edited a number of books, including *Old High German Literature*. He has contributed articles, poems, and reviews to numerous scholarly journals and literary magazines.

Bibliography

"*All Quiet* Arouses German Critics' Ire," *New York Times* (6 December 1930).

"*All Quiet on the Western Front*," *New Statesman* (25 May 1929): 218.

"*All Quiet on the Western Front*," *Times Literary Supplement* (August 4, 1929): 314.

Baumer, Franz. *E. M. Remarque*. Berlin: Colloquium Verlag, 1976.

Bergonzi, Bernard. *Heroes' Twilight: A Study of the Literature of the Great War*. New York: Coward McCann, 1966.

Bithell, Jethro. *Modern German Literature, 1880–1950*. London: Methuen & Co. Ltd., 1959.

Bonadeo, Alfredo. "War and Degradation: Gleanings from the Literature of the Great War," *Comparative Literature Studies* (Winter 1984): 408–33.

Bostock, J. Knight. *Some Well-Known German War Novels 1914–1930*. Oxford: B. H. Blackwell Ltd., 1931.

Brooks, Cyrus. "Herr Remarque Shuns Literary Honors," *New York Times Magazine*, (22 September 1929): 7.

Canby, Henry Seidel. "Modern War," *Saturday Review of Literature* (8 June 1929): 1027.

Cernyak, Susan E. "The Life of a Nation: The Community of the Dispossessed in E. M. Remarque's Emigration Novels," *Perspectives on Contemporary Literature* (1977): 15–22.

Duesberg, W. "Telephoning Remarque," *Living Age* 340 (June 1931): 372–75.

Eksteins, Modris. "*All Quiet on the Western Front* and the Fate of a War," *Journal of Contemporary History* (April 1980): 345–65.

———. *Rites of Spring: The Great War and the Birth of the Modern Age*. Boston: Houghton Mifflin, 1989.

Eloesser, Arthur. *Modern German Literature*, translated by Catherine Alison Phillips. New York: Alfred Knopf, 1933.

Emmel, Hildegard. "The Novel during the Weimar Republic." In *History of the German Novel*. Detroit: Wayne State University Press, 1984.

The Erich Maria Remarque Collection. In the Remarque Room, Fales Library, at New York University.

161

"Erich Maria Remarque, Violent Author . . . Quiet Man," *Newsweek* (1 April 1957): 108–9.

Fussell, Paul. *The Great War and Modern Memory*. New York: Oxford University Press, 1975.

Garland, Henry and Mary. *The Oxford Companion to German Literature*. Oxford: Clarendon Press, 1976.

Gay, Peter. *Weimar Culture: The Outsider as Insider*. New York: Harper and Row, 1968.

"The Great Adventure. Why Paul Baumer Died," *The (London) Observer* (10 October 1929): 13–14.

Hagbolt, P. "Ethical and Social Problems in the German War Novel," *Journal of English and German Philology* 32 (1933): 21–32.

Hamilton, Ian. "The End of War?: A Correspondence between the Author of *All Quiet on the Western Front* and General Sir Ian Hamilton," *Life and Letters* 3 (November 1929): 399.

Hill, Frank Ernest, "Destroyed by the War," *New York Herald Tribune*, Books section, (June 2, 1929).

Hoffmann, Charles W. "Erich Maria Remarque." In *German Fiction Writers, 1914–1945*, ed., James Hardin. Detroit: Gale Research, 1987.

Kamla, Thomas A. *Confrontation with Exile: Studies in the German Novel*. Bern: Herbert Land, 1975.

Krispyn, Egbert. *Anti-Nazi Writers in Exile*. Athens: University of Georgia Press, 1978.

Last, Rex. "The 'Castration' of Erich Maria Remarque," *Quinquereme* 2 (1979): 10–22.

Lefèvre, Frédéric. "An Hour with Erich Remarque," Living Age 339 (December 1930): 344.

Marton, Ruth. "Remarque's First Novels," *New York Times Book Review* (3 February 1986).

"The Meaning of Exile," *Time* (April 18 1941): 91–92.

Murdoch, Brian. "'All Quiet on the Trojan Front': Remarque, Homer and War as the Targets of Literary Parody," *German Life and Letters* (October 1989): 49–62.

Murdoch, Brian, Mark Ward, and Maggie Sargeant, eds. *Remarque against War. Essays for the Centenary of Erich Maria Remarque, 1898–1970*. Glasgow: Scottish Papers in Germanic Studies, 1998.

Ossietzky, Carl von. "The Remarque Case," transl. John Peet. In *The Stolen Republic: Selected Writings of Carl von Ossietzky*, ed. Bruno Frei. Berlin: Seven Seas Publishers, 1971.

Owen, C. R. *Erich Maria Remarque: A Critical Bio-Bibliography*. Atlantic Highlands, New Jersey: Humanities, 1984.

Read, Herbert. "Books of the Quarter," *Criterion* (April 1929).

———. "German War Books," *Manchester Guardian Weekly* (26 April 1929): 335.

———. "A Lost Generation," *The Nation and Athenaeum* 45 (27 April 1929): 116.

Riddick, John F. "Erich Maria Remarque: A Bibliography of Biographical and Critical Material, 1929–1980," *Bulletin of Bibliography* (December 1982): 207–10.

Rowley, Brian A. "Journalism into Fiction: *Im Westen nichts Neues*." In *The First World War in Fiction: A Collection of Critical Essays*, ed. Holger Klein. London: Macmillan, 1976.

Simmons, Jerold, "Film and International Politics: The Banning of *All Quiet on the Western Front* in Germany and Austria, 1930–1931," *Historian* (November 1989).

Taylor, Harley U., Jr. "Autobiographical Elements in the Novels of Erich Maria Remarque," *West Virginia University Philological Papers* (1970): 84–93.

———. *Erich Maria Remarque: A Literary and Film Biography*. New York: Peter Lang, 1989.

van Gelder, R. "An Interview with Remarque," In *Writers and Writing*. New York: Charles Scribner's & Sons, 1946.

"Volume Expurgated on Book Club Advice . . . Toned down for Americans," *New York Times* (31 May 1929).

Waidson, H. M. *The Modern German Novel*. London: Oxford University Press, 1959.

Wagener, Hans. "Erich Maria Remarque: Shadows in Paradise." In *Exile: The Writer's Experience*, Spalek, John M. and Robert F. Bell, eds. Chapel Hill: University of North Carolina Press, 1982.

Acknowledgments

"Remarque and Other Men of Feeling" by William K. Pfeiler. From *War and the German Mind: The Testimony of Men of Fiction Who Fought at the Front.* © 1941 Columbia University Press. Reprinted by permission.

"Christ As Doomed Youth: Remarque's *All Quiet on the Western Front*" by Edwin M. Moseley. From *Pseudonyms of Christ in the Modern Novel: Motifs and Methods.* © 1962 by the University of Pittsburgh. Reprinted by permission of University of Pittsburgh Press.

"Two War Novels: A Critical Comparison" by Helmut Liedloff. From *Revue de Littérature comparée* 42, no. 3 (July–September 1968). © 1968 Centre National de la Recherche Scientifique. Reprinted by permission.

"The Works of Ernst Jünger and Erich Maria Remarque on World War I" by Wilhelm J. Schwarz. From *War and the Mind of Germany.* © 1975 Herbert Lang & Co. Ltd. and Peter Lang Ltd. Reprinted by permission.

"'Im Westen nichts Neues': A Bestseller in Context" by A. F. Bance. From *The Modern Language Review* 72 (1977). © 1977 Modern Humanities Research Association. Reprinted by permission.

"*All Quiet on the Western Front*" by Christine R. Barker and R. W. Last. From *Erich Maria Remarque.* © 1979 Oswald Wolff (Publishers) Ltd. Reprinted by permission of Barnes and Noble.

"Liberal Education on the Western Front" by Roland Garrett. From *The Journal of General Education* 31, no. 3 (Fall 1979): 151–57. © 1979 The Pennsylvania State University. Reprinted by permission of The Pennsylvania State University Press.

"All Quiet on the Western Front" by Hans Wagener. From *Understanding Erich Maria Remarque.* © 1991 University of South Carolina. Reprinted by permission.

"Die Front ist ein Käfig: Paul Bäumer's War" by Brian O. Murdoch. From *Remarque: Im Westen nichts Neues.* © 1995 University of Glasgow French and German Publications. Reprinted by permission.

Index